SCHOLASTIC

SCHOLASTIC GO GRAMMAR

Course Book

Level 4

Additional illustrations by Durgadatt Pandey

Published by Scholastic India Pvt. Ltd.
A subsidiary of Scholastic Inc., New York, 10012 (USA).
Publishers since 1920, with international operations in Canada, Australia, New Zealand, the United Kingdom, India, and Hong Kong.

For information regarding permission, write to:
Scholastic India Pvt. Ltd.
A-27, Ground Floor, Bharti Sigma Centre
Infocity-1, Sector 34, Gurgaon (Haryana) 122001
Email: info_in@scholastic.asia

Typeset at Digital Expressions

First edition: 2008
Reprinted: 2009 (thrice), 2010, 2011 (four times), 2012 (thrice), 2013 (twice), 2014 (twice), 2015 (thrice), 2016 (thrice), 2017 (thrice), 2018 (thrice), 2019 (twice), 2020, 2021, 2022, 2023 (twice), 2024, 2025, 2026

ISBN-13: 978-81-8477-147-3

Contents

Thank You!

The *Go Grammar* **books were sent out to approximately eighty schools across the country for primary school principals, departmental heads and teachers to give their feedback on the contents. The publishers would like to thank all those who took the time out of their busy schedules to go through the books and make many valuable suggestions, which have been duly incorporated.**

Alaukika Khachar, The Rajkumar College, Rajkot
Alka Kshetrapal, Delhi Public School, Bilaspur
Anjana Henry, Delhi Public School, Bilaspur
Anuradha Tandan, Seth Anandram Jaipuria School, Kanpur
Arpita Mitra, Delhi Public School, Bilaspur
Caroline O Conner, Delhi Public School, Bilaspur
Denise Wesley, Delhi Public School, Bilaspur
G. Annapurna, Delhi Public School, Bilaspur
Hemavathi, N.S.N Matric Hr Sec School, Chennai
Indrani Ganguly, St. John's Whitehall Secondary School, Shillong
Madhu Hora, Seth Anandram Jaipuria School, Kanpur
Manisha Francis, Delhi Public School, Bilaspur
Manju Negi, R.D. Rajpal Public School, New Delhi
Manu Mishra, Delhi Public School, Bilaspur
Mathew Panamkat, Doon Public School, Delhi
Maushumi Deb, St. John's Whitehall Secondary School, Shillong
Maya Shukla, Delhi Public School, Bilaspur
Monisha Bhattacharya, Julien Day School, Kolkata
N. Sambasivarao, Pragathi Vidya Niketan, Hyderabad
Neha Jain, Gyan Bharati School, New Delhi
P. Nirmala, Delhi Public School, Vishakapatnam
Payal Dubey, Seth Anandram Jaipuria School, Kanpur
R. Niranjani, Chinmaya Vidyalaya, Anna Nagar, Chennai
Radhika Wadhwa, Gyan Bharati School, New Delhi
Renu Vashishta, Maharana Mewar Vidya Mandir, Udaipur
Renuka Semwal, Gyan Bharati School, New Delhi
Reshmi Sarkar, R.D. Rajpal Public School, New Delhi
S. Haldia, MGD Girls School, Jaipur
Sagarika Satpathy, Delhi Public School, Vishakapatnam
Sandeep Mishra, Delhi Public School, Bilaspur
Sangeeta Bali, R.D. Rajpal Public School, New Delhi
Shobha Gopakumar, Delhi Public School, Vishakapatnam
Sonia Abraham, Delhi Public School, Bilaspur
Sujatha, N.S.N Matric Hr Sec School, Chennai
Sulekha Bhattacharya, St. John's Whitehall Secondary School, Shillong
The English Department Co-ordinator, Delhi Public School, Dwarka, New Delhi
Usha Sankar, N.S.N Matric Hr Sec School, Chennai
Vandana Pathak, Delhi Public School, Vishakapatnam
Vasanti Tank, The Rajkumar College, Rajkot

Special thanks to Sunita Malkani for her assistance and advice.

In addition to the people listed above, there were many teachers who did not want their help to be publicly acknowledged. In deference to their wishes, we have not included their names, but we would once again like to acknowledge their valuable help.

Introduction

Go Grammar is a series of English grammar course books for the primary classes. The books have been created by a panel of eminent authors, school and college teachers, and experienced children's publishers. They have been vetted by school teachers and principals from different parts of India. The approach follows the current NCERT curriculum and pedagogical principles.

Grammar is the heart and soul of language. An understanding of grammar gives mastery and control over all forms of communication, both verbal and written. Students need to develop the skills to express themselves creatively and meaningfully. These books are intended to help students build a strong and solid foundation in language usage.

The *Go Grammar* books cover the following topics:

- Nouns
- Adjectives
- Verbs
- Adverbs
- Tenses
- Prepositions
- Articles
- Conjunctions
- Sentences

For in-depth understanding of the concepts, the book includes the following features:

Read with Your Teacher: This section introduces each topic, giving definitions and examples. With every successive level, it recapitulates what has been taught before and introduces more complex details. Teachers can either choose to start by reading this section with their students when beginning a new topic, or use it as a revision exercise after the chapter has been completed.

Games: The Read with Your Teacher section also includes individual and team activities to reinforce the concepts in a fun manner and to give the students essential verbal practice.

Worksheets: The concepts learnt can be further strengthened through exercise sheets which can be worked on at school or at home. The fun activities and attractive illustrations engage the students' attention and enhance the learning experience.

Composition: This section helps students improve their writing skills. The activities are designed to encourage students to use grammatically correct language. Writing notices, diary entries, messages, paragraphs, book reviews, letters and notes gives students the confidence to use the language effectively and practically.

Revision tests: This thoughtfully planned section helps the students review and evaluate their progress on the concepts they have learnt.

Word banks: The extensive lists of antonyms, homophones, compound words, collective nouns, suffixes and prefixes help improve vocabulary and reinforce the learning.

An informative and motivating set of books, *Go Grammar* will help students apply the rules of grammar in spoken and written English, to make them effective and articulate communicators.

Nouns

Recap

Nouns are words that name people, places, animals and things in a sentence.
Different nouns have different jobs to do.

Common nouns name everyday things around us.
Proper nouns give people, places, objects and events their given or special names.
Singular nouns name one thing.
Plural nouns name more than one thing.
Most plural nouns are formed by adding **s** or **es** to the singular noun.
Some plurals are formed by changing the vowels or adding **en.**
For example: foot—feet, man—men, child—children
Some nouns are both singular and plural.
For example: sheep, fish, deer
Some nouns are only plural.
For example: trousers, scissors, cutlery, crockery

Gender nouns

You have learnt about masculine and feminine nouns. The common gender is names of people that can be either male or female.
For example: writer, doctor.
The neuter gender is when a noun is neither male nor female.
For example: table, chair

Compound nouns are made by joining two words together.
For example: snowflake, heartbeat, tablecloth, sandcastle, penknife, butterscotch, basketball

Possessive nouns show ownership. An apostrophe is always used.
For example: Jack's horse; the teacher's book; the cats' whiskers

Collective nouns are names given to groups of persons or things.
For example: flock (of birds); herd (of cows); crowd (of people)

Nouns

Concrete and abstract nouns

A concrete noun names a person, animal, place or thing that you can actually see, touch, taste, hear or smell.

Abstract nouns deal with things we cannot see, hear, smell or touch. An abstract noun names an idea, a feeling, a quality or an action.

For example: bravery, wisdom, youth, courage, affection

Countable and Uncountable Nouns

Countable nouns are things that we can count.

For example: pencil. We can count pencils. We can have one, two, three or more pencils.

- Countable nouns can be singular or plural.
- We can use a few and many with countable nouns.

For example: I've got a few dollars. I haven't got many eggs.

People is a countable noun. **People** is the plural of person and we can count persons.

Uncountable nouns are items or concepts that we cannot divide into separate elements. We cannot count them.

For example: we cannot count **water**. We can count **bottles of water** or **litres of water** but we cannot count water itself. Examples of uncountable nouns are music, furniture, luggage, sugar, gas, money.

We usually treat uncountable nouns as singular.

For example, the furniture is made of teak wood.

We can use some, any, a little and much with uncountable nouns.

Nouns

Games

- ### Feel and Find

  Fill a cloth bag with a variety of small objects. Have the students feel the outside of the bag to see if they can identify any objects. They can write the names of the things on a sheet of paper.

- ### Letter Fun

  Challenge the students to write a common noun for every letter of the alphabet. You can set a time limit for this activity. For example: A = apricot, B = berry, C = cherry. You can also ask them to provide names of fruits or towns with the letters.

- ### Add the Words

  Review some examples of compound nouns with the students. Ask them to provide examples of compound nouns with the following combinations:

  Noun + noun (bedroom, watertank, motorcycle)

  Noun + verb (haircut, rainfall)

  Adjective + noun (greenhouse, redhead, software)

- ### Imaginary Collectives

  After discussing common collective nouns, such as a flock of birds, a herd of cattle, ask the students to make up their own imaginary collective nouns that they feel would suit a group of creatures.

  For example: a hop of frogs, a slither of snakes, a trumpet of elephants

Nouns

Common nouns name everyday things around us. Proper nouns give specific names to objects, places and events.

1 Read the story below and underline the common and proper nouns and circle the neuter, common, masculine and feminine nouns.

Birbal was Emperor Akbar's favourite minister. Akbar enjoyed his company because Birbal was a clever man with great common sense.

One day Akbar said to Birbal, "I am amazed at your belief that God comes to earth in the form of a human being."

"Nothing to marvel at. He is the father of the universe," said Birbal.

"Why should the creator spoil his Divine Form and jump into the Ocean of Life?" asked Akbar. Birbal was silent.

A few days later, Akbar and Birbal were walking along the bank of Yamuna. Akbar's youngest grandson was on the knees of his beautiful nurse in a boat. The nurse got up to wish Akbar and the child fell into the river. Akbar immediately jumped into the river to save the little boy. Swimming fast he reached the floating child. To his amazement it was a doll that fell off the boat.

Birbal said, "You did not worry about your royal form and jumped to rescue the child. This is similar to the way God loves the children of the earth and is always ready to help us."

Singular and Plural Nouns

Singular nouns name one thing.
Plural nouns name more than one thing.

1 Write the form (**S**-singular or **P**-plural) for the underlined nouns.

a I found a lot of flowers in the garden. ________ ________

b Many people were standing in the queue for the office to open. ________

c The child ate the cherry. ________ ________

d We saw lions, tigers and monkeys in the zoo. ________ ________

e The men chased the thief. ________ ________

f The bees flew away when Neeraj lit a fire. ________ ________

g The fox was hiding in the bush. ________ ________

h The knives are sharp. ________

i My tooth is hurting. ________

j The women went to see the butterflies. ________ ________

k The sheep were in the field. ________ ________

l My uncle's wife lives in a big building. ________ ________

m Tomatoes and potatoes are available easily. ________ ________

2 Fill in the blanks with **much** or **many**.

a How ______________ people live in your city?

b How ______________ money do you have?

c How ______________ teachers will come?

d How ______________ rice do we need?

e How ______________ does that dress cost?

f How ______________ times did you see the movie?

Compound Nouns

A compound noun is made up of two words joined together, for example: cornflakes, football, footprints, streetlight.

1 **Choose a word in the top row and one in the bottom to make a compound noun. Colour the compound nouns, using a different colour for each one.**

post	hair	pigeon	drain	sun	drum	tooth
flowers	hole	pick	card	stick	pipe	brush

2 **Write sentences using these compound nouns:**

masterpiece *cornstalks* *spotlight* *passers-by* *riverbank*

____

____

____

____

____

3 **Join the two words that make a compound noun.**

a	hay	shelf	____________
b	fence	storm	____________
c	hair	post	____________
d	thunder	stack	*haystack*
e	book	beans	____________
f	jelly	piece	____________

4 **How many compound words can you make by putting two of these words together? All words can be used more than once. Write a minimum of 20 words. Decide who has the record for the most words.**

fire	river	line	farm	way	bush	water
place	head	bed	house	light	clothes	land
room	side	hill	life	under	time	top

WORK SHEET 4

Collective Nouns

Collective nouns name groups of people or things, for example: a herd of goats, a fleet of ships, a school of fish.

1 Living things usually live and move together in groups. Match these animals with their groups.

lions *monkeys* *cubs* *whales* *elephants* *wolves* *fish* *geese*

a a herd of ______________________

b a school of ______________________

c a troop of ______________________

d a pod of ______________________

e a pack of ______________________

f a flock of ______________________

g a litter of ______________________

h a pride of ______________________

2 Circle the collective nouns in this passage.

Up in the rafters of our hayshed lives a family of pigeons, while below, amongst the straw, Bessie watches over her litter of tiny white kittens. In one paddock we have a flock of sheep. Dad keeps a watchful eye on them, because of the pack of wild dogs that sometimes roam the hills. We have a large herd of cows, which are brought in for milking twice a day. Occasionally, we see a flock of wild ducks fly overhead on their way to the waterhole.

3 Complete and search out the collective nouns.

a litter of p______________

a herd of e________________

a brood of ch______________

a shoal of f______________

a mob of k________________

a flock of sh__________

a swarm of b_______

a pride of l__________

a troop of m ______________

a crowd of p______________

T	B	R	A	L	P	G	Y	H	E
E	L	E	P	H	A	N	T	S	C
F	J	I	K	M	O	T	J	I	H
S	N	L	P	L	Z	P	M	F	I
H	Y	I	E	B	X	S	O	T	C
E	S	O	O	R	A	G	N	A	K
E	R	N	P	L	W	I	K	U	E
P	G	S	L	Q	V	P	E	H	N
K	I	B	E	E	S	T	Y	D	S
R	P	U	P	P	I	E	S	T	D

WORK SHEET 5

Possessive Nouns

Possessive nouns show ownership. We use an apostrophe to show possession. For example:
Claire's shoes, cat's whiskers, boy's hat, hen's feathers, teachers' books.

If there is one owner, just add **'s**.	If there is more than one owner, put an apostrophe after the plural noun.	If the plural noun does NOT end in s, add **'s**.

The man's hat *(the hat belonging to the man)*	The girls' cats *(the cats belonging to the girls)*	The children's kites *(the kites belonging to the children)*

1 Rewrite each sentence using apostrophes to show possession.

a The horse belongs to Dinesh. It is Dinesh's horse.

b The car belongs to Mr Tapan. It ______________________

c The web belongs to a spider. It ______________________

d The bones belong to dinosaurs. They are ______________________

e The nests belong to birds. They ______________________

f The scarves belong to the men. They ______________________

2 Who owns the objects that are underlined in these sentences?

a It is the builder's toolbox. *the builder*

b Owls' eyes peered in the dark. ______________________

c There is the farmer's field. ______________________

d We ate the women's cakes. ______________________

e I patted my friend's dogs. ______________________

f These are Aditya's shorts. ______________________

3 Write a sentence about the dragons' cave OR the witch's frogs.

____

Possessive Nouns - Singular

Possessive nouns name the single owners of things, for example: Ankita's bucket, Jim's book, the boy's dirty hands. **You will need an apostrophe. Use 's for single owners.**

TIP: Ask who is the owner? – THAT is where you put the apostrophe.

1 Highlight the possessive nouns.

a Where is Rohit's football?

b I put on Tania's watch by mistake.

c That is Ajay's model plane.

d What is Jess' last name?

e My brother's new car is a Ferrari.

NOTE: If the owner ends in s, just add an apostrophe.

2 Use apostrophes to show ownership.

a Mum found my brother____ socks in Dad____ sock drawer.

b This is my aunt and uncle____ old stone farmhouse.

c Which is Tessa____ house?

d Sam made a pirate____ sword, and I made a knight____ shield.

e Is this schoolbag Ben____ or Eric____?

f Jai and Omar____ lunchboxes are exactly the same.

If there are two different owners, add 's after the second owner.

3 Write 3 sentences. Choose from the following subjects:

parrot's feathers *river's edge* *player's injuries*
magician's wand *farmer's cows* *Ramesh's violin*

____

____

____

____

____

____

Possessive Nouns - Plural

Possessive nouns name the plural owners of things, for example: zebras' stripes, four dogs' bones, the boys' muddy clothes. **You will need an apostrophe. Place the apostrophe after the plural owners.**

TIP: Ask who is the owner? – THAT is where you put the apostrophe.

1 Are the owners singular or plural?

a Dad buys dogs' bones once a week. ____________

b Jockeys' shirts are made of colourful silks. ____________

c David's remote-controlled car is very fast. ____________

d Birds' feathers lay scattered below the tree. ____________

e I climbed onto the horse's back and off she trotted. ____________

2 Add apostrophes correctly to show ownership.

a We heard the beat of eagles wings.

b Most of the citys buildings were damaged in the storm.

c The cars tyre is flat.

d All the swimmers times have improved with training.

e Elephants tusks are made of ivory.

If the plural noun is irregular, just add ***'s***, for example: *children's toys, men's golf clubs, women's shoes.*

3 Who owns the objects that are underlined?

a It is the builder's toolbox. *builder*

b Owls' eyes peered in the dark. ____________

c He's in the teachers' staffroom. ____________

d She designs women's clothes. ____________

e I soaked up the sun's warmth. ____________

f These are Tom's shorts. ____________

g There's a ribbon on the lady's hat. ____________

h Look at the babies' photos. ____________

i You'll find men's shoes on that shelf. ____________

j The cars' windows are dirty. ____________

Abstract Nouns

A concrete noun is a person, animal or thing that you can see or touch. An abstract noun tells us about things we cannot hear, see or touch.

1 Fill in the blanks with the following abstract nouns.

amazement	honesty	cleanliness	wisdom	greed

a The sages of ancient times were full of ____________.

b _________ is the best policy.

c To his ___________ he jumped into the river.

d _________ is a deadly sin.

e ____________ is next to godliness.

2 Write the correct adjectives of the following abstract nouns.

a height ____________

b strength ____________

c warmth ____________

d weakness ____________

e bravery ____________

f darkness ____________

g kindness ____________

h width ____________

i sadness ____________

j cruelty ____________

3 Pick out some abstract nouns from the following puzzle.
One is done for you.

ATMPGS<u>ADNESS</u>VRLDHSGYWISDOMUVJT

RLGDPLOTRUTHMLJUSTICELHFEARBHYT

XLNLOVEESVTMPJKRBLDYOUTHASFTRG

MJCHILDHOODSRTYHJGREEDLKJTGKNVL

Abstract Nouns

Nouns that name our thoughts and feelings are called abstract nouns, for example: hope, anger, love, disappointment, greed, beauty, tolerance. **You cannot see or touch abstract ideas – they exist in your thoughts and in your feelings.**

1 Circle only the nouns that name abstract ideas.

sorrow	porcupine	glamour	clarinet	chieftain
hope	anger	lantern	container	tolerance
happiness	laundry	despair	chalk	grief

2 Find and circle the abstract nouns in these sentences.

a We watched in despair as the dam levels dropped lower and lower.

b It was such a disappointment when our team lost the match.

c The story tells of great moments of sadness and of happiness.

d The searchers gave up all hope of finding the missing boy before nightfall.

e With longing in his heart, the puppy watched the people passing the pet shop.

3 Write three sentences beginning with these abstract feelings.

a In a fit of anger ______________________________

b In a voice filled with fear, ______________________________

c With great excitement, ______________________________

4 Write three sentences about these abstract thoughts:

honesty confidence greed

____

____

____

____

____

____

Countable and Uncountable Nouns

Countable nouns are things we can count. Uncountable nouns are items that cannot be separated into their elements and counted.

1 **Tick (√) the countable nouns and cross (x) the uncountable nouns.**

a bottles ☐	*g* dirt ☐	*m* steel ☐
b fish ☐	*h* pens ☐	*n* coins ☐
c iron ☐	*i* grass ☐	*o* smoke ☐
d air ☐	*j* butter ☐	*p* news ☐
e flour ☐	*k* money ☐	*q* holes ☐
f books ☐	*l* rivers ☐	*r* bead ☐

2 **Fill in the blanks with a few, a lot of, much, many, a little.**

a There is ________ water in the well because there has not been ______ rain.

b I could not buy apples in the store because there were only ________ left.

c There isn't ________ petrol in the scooter.

d Try ________ of the vegetable curry.

e He doesn't find _____ time for walking these days as he has _________ work to do.

f He drank ________ lemonade, but did not eat _______ food.

g She took ________ sweets from the box. There are still _______ left.

h How _______ more money do you want?

i Go and put _______ powder on your face.

j The bus will be here in _________ minutes.

Adjectives

Adjectives are words that give colour, shape, size, sound and feeling to nouns. They paint a clearer picture of the nouns.
For example: I had a juicy orange.
My dog has soft, brown fur.

Adjectives of degree may describe nouns as they are (positive degree).
For example: I have a long rope
Or compared to another (comparative degree)
For example: My rope is longer than yours
Or compared to all others (superlative degree)
For example: Todd has the longest rope of all

- Suffixes **–er** and **–est** are usually used to make adjectives of degree. Some adjectives add **–er** or **–est** without any change in their spellings.
  For example: old, older, oldest
  sweet, sweeter, sweetest
- Adjectives that end in **–e** drop the **–e** when adding **–er** or **–est.**
  For example: large, larger, largest

Other adjectives of degree are formed by placing **more** or **most** before the adjective.
More and most are used before adjectives that already end in a suffix.
For example: beautiful, more beautiful, most beautiful
helpful, more helpful, most helpful

Different adjectives have different jobs to do.
Descriptive adjectives give colour, shape, size and feelings to nouns.
Verbal adjectives are participles used as adjectives. Participles end in **-ing** or **–ed.**
For example: a walking stick, falling rocks, a puzzled look, a dazed expression
Number adjectives give quantity to the noun.
For example: ten eggs, sixth person, first place

Adjectives

Antonyms

Adjectives describe nouns. Adjectives also show opposite ways of describing nouns.

Antonyms are adjectives with opposite meanings.

For example: dull/bright day, sweet/sour oranges, rough/smooth road, fresh/stale cake, short/tall man

Demonstrative adjectives

Demonstrative adjectives point out particular persons or things. **This**, **these**, **that**, **those** are demonstrative adjectives.

For example: This boy is thin. Those books on the shelf are old.

Games

- ### Adding to the Story

  Write a short story or a joke on the blackboard. Underline all the nouns. Have the students rewrite the story by adding adjectives to the nouns.

  Two caterpillars were eating grass when a butterfly flew overhead.

  Two large fat caterpillars were eating green, delicious grass ...

- ### Know Your Friends

  Have students describe each other using positive adjectives.

  For example: Shruti is an honest girl.
  Rohit is a fast runner.

- ### Antonym Game

  Divide the class into two teams. One team will call out an adjective and the other team will give the opposite of the adjective.

  For example: right/wrong, useful/useless, stop/start

- ### Adding Nouns

  Give students a list of adjectives and ask them to add suitable nouns.

  curly ____________
  delicious ____________
  sharp ____________
  three ____________

Adjectives of Degree

Adjectives of degree describe how people and things compare with each other. They show how much more or less, for example: John is tall. Omar is taller. Mohit is tallest.
To show degree we usually add –er and –est.

1 Colour the matching adjectives of degree.

Positive	*Comparative*	*Superlative*
loud	wetter	strongest
tall	thinner	loudest
fierce	louder	fiercest
wet	stronger	wettest
thin	fiercer	tallest
strong	taller	thinnest

2 Complete the table of adjectives of degree.

Positive	*Comparative*	*Superlative*
long	longer	longest
old		
sharp		
wild		
soft		
brave		

3 Complete the adjectives of degree correctly. Add *–er* or *–est*.

a That was the cold______ day in winter.

b It is hott______ today than it was yesterday.

c My grandma is old______ than yours.

d Jayant is the fast______ runner in our class.

e The red box is large, but the blue one is larg______.

4 Some adjectives of degree are not formed by adding –er and –est. For example: *good, better, best* and *bad, worse, worst.* Write two sentences to include some of these adjectives.

a ____

b ____

WORK SHEET 12

Adjectives of Degree

Some adjectives of degree are formed by adding more or most before the adjective. Suffixes -er and -est are used to make adjectives of degree.

1 Complete the box.

Positive	*Comparative*	*Superlative*
careful		
rich		
wonderful		
good		
enjoyable		
deep		

2 Fill in the blanks with the correct degree of adjectives.

a Today is ____________ than yesterday. (cold)

b For Sunita mathematics is ____________, English is ____________, but science is the ____________ of all. (difficult).

c Who is ____________, you or your sister? (old)

d Which is the ____________ dress in the shop? (expensive)

e The king wanted to build a palace, ____________ than any in the world. (large)

f The days are ____________ in winters. (short)

3 Some adjectives of degree are not formed by adding –er and –est.

For example: *good, better, best; bad, worse, worst; many, more, most; little, less, least.*

Use the correct adjective to complete these sentences.

a The coach told us it was the ________ game we had played this season.

b He told us that we must do ________ next time.

c He really wanted us to be the ________ team in the district.

d However, things went from ________ to ________.

e By the end of the season, our team had the ________ number of points.

Demonstrative Adjectives

Demonstrative adjectives indicate specific items. Instead of referring to the shirt, we can point out to one particular shirt as this shirt or that shirt.

1 Fill in the blanks with the correct demonstrative adjectives.

a Whose books are ________?

b We have seen ________ exotic flowers before.

c "Leave ________ house," said Ravi.

d ________ houses there are made of black bricks.

e I am sure you can win ________ championship.

f ________ house on the mountain looks small, but it is really a mansion.

g ________ are my books.

h What do you think about ________?

i Why don't we go to ________ doctor?

j ________ children are very naughty.

k ________ is the dress I was talking about.

l ________ apples are raw. Buy ________ ones.

m ________ cap in the bag is not mine.

n I can't go there wearing ________ dress.

WORK SHEET 14

Verbal Adjectives

Some forms of the verb can be used as adjectives. They are called verbal adjectives. They end in –ing or –ed, for example:
a walking stick, falling rocks, a winding road, loaded trucks, a puzzled look.

1 Join these verbal adjectives to the nouns they describe.

a dancing	rocks		*g* scented	shoes
b an exciting	clouds		*h* loaded	dinner
c swimming	book		*i* baked	cream
d falling	shoes		*j* polished	rose
e an interesting	costume		*k* spotted	truck
f floating	day		*l* whipped	deer

2 Use three of the noun groups given above in sentences.

a ______________________________

b ______________________________

c ______________________________

3 Make a sketch of each noun group.

a smiling clown	a parked car	splashing waves	a potted plant
a skipping rope	a painted face	a walking stick	a speckled hen

WORK SHEET 15

Verbal Adjectives

Some forms of the verb can be used as adjectives. They are called verbal adjectives. They end in –ing or –ed, for example:
a walking stick, falling rocks, a winding road, loaded trucks, a puzzled look.

1 Join these verbal adjectives to the nouns they describe.

a	a chiming	wind	*g* roasted	truck
b	exciting	vehicle	*h* a haunted	jumper
c	a wailing	news	*i* a knitted	cacti
d	puzzling	clock	*j* branded	peanuts
e	a howling	questions	*k* a bogged	house
f	a speeding	siren	*l* potted	cattle

2 Build sentences around five noun groups of your choice.

____

____

____

____

____

3 Choose a verbal adjective in the top line to describe a noun on the bottom line. Colour each pair the same colour.

melted	walking	setting	knotted	dancing	boiled	preserved	laughing
shoes	rope	butter	eggs	fruit	stick	clown	sun

painted	growing	chewing	ploughed	gaping	bundled	cooked	cheering
sticks	meat	fence	crowd	plants	field	gum	hole

Antonyms

Adjectives can describe people and things in opposite ways, for example: happy face – sad face; old books – new books; a long road – a short road.

1 Write antonyms for these adjectives.

a expensive ____________ *d* narrow ____________ *g* dark ____________

b high ____________ *e* fresh ____________ *h* long ____________

c smooth ____________ *f* empty ____________ *i* ugly ____________

2 Now complete these sentences by using the correct antonyms.

a Because of the drought, fruit that was once ________ is now ________.

b The tanks were ________, but now they are ________.

c The hikers emerged from the ________ cave into ________ sunlight.

d Rivers are ________, but creeks are ________.

e The ____________ swan swam away from the ________ toad.

f Do you want a ________ or a ________ piece of string?

g The bread is ________, but the buns are ________.

3 Search out the antonyms of the adjectives in the list.

old ____________

large ____________

wrong ____________

wild ____________

top ____________

new ____________

hot ____________

small ____________

heavy ____________

tall ____________

wet ____________

clean ____________

S	T	P	S	N	C	J	O	K	W
D	A	B	H	L	D	R	Y	L	E
Y	M	G	O	L	D	P	O	H	N
U	E	N	R	O	Z	B	U	G	L
D	I	R	T	Y	B	I	G	U	P
S	T	I	E	L	L	I	G	H	T
H	E	G	R	A	L	T	M	R	L
O	F	H	E	P	A	W	G	J	K
B	O	T	T	O	M	A	Y	P	N
S	R	O	P	X	S	D	L	O	C

Antonyms

Adding certain prefixes or suffixes can also form antonyms, for example: appear – disappear; possible – impossible; helpful – helpless.

Prefixes that form antonyms include: *dis-, un-, in-, im-, il-, ir-, mis-*
Suffixes that form antonyms include: *-ful, -less*

1 Add a prefix to show adjectives of opposite meaning.

a The journalist was ____armed as he went into the battle zone.

b The ____literate man signed his name, but it was ____possible to read.

c It is highly ____ likely that Jonathan will be ____obedient.

d Our coach made the ____accurate statement that our team was ____beatable.

e It was an ____believable sight! The comet was suddenly ____visible.

2 Complete this table of antonyms.

	-ful	-less
a help		
b use		
c care		
d hope		
e pain		

	-ful	-less
f thought		
g colour		
h power		
i doubt		
j cheer		

3 Highlight the correct adjective in each pair.

a The river was flowing so swiftly, we were (powerful, powerless) to help.

b It is (probable, improbable) that man will one day live on the moon.

c It is (legal, illegal) to park in a bus stop.

d I had the (fortune, misfortune) to win first prize in the competition.

e Your answer is (correct, incorrect). You will need to try again.

f I'm sure he will be here soon. He is very (reliable, unreliable).

g Thank you for waiting for me. You are most (thoughtful, thoughtless).

h It was very (responsible, irresponsible) to leave your young sister behind.

Verbs

Verbs consist of one or more words that show the particular interactions and relationships between people, places, events and objects.

Different verbs have different jobs to do.
Doing verbs show the actions of people and things. For example: fly, swim, sleep
Being verbs show that people and things exist. For example: am, is, are, were
Having verbs show what people and things have. For example: have, had, having
Saying verbs show how living things (or personified objects) express themselves. For example: growl, call, shout, cry
Helping verbs are used with present and past participles to make a complete verb. Their job is to show tense and possibility.
For example: We are eating dinner. They were eating chips.

Contractions

We often contract verb and (pronoun) subject.
For example: I am = I'm; it is = it's; they are = they're
We often contract verb and negative.
For example: will not = won't; cannot = can't; did not = didn't

Subject-Verb agreement

Rules:

- If the subject is plural, a plural verb is required.

For example: The boys are coming down the road.
The girls like chocolates.

- If the subject is singular, a singular verb is required.

For example: The boy is coming down the road.
The girl likes chocolates.

- If there is more than one subject joined by **and**, a plural verb is required.

For example: Here come the bride and groom.

- Collective nouns usually take a singular verb.

For example: A bunch of grapes
An army of frogs

Verbs

Games

- ### Fill in the Blanks

On the blackboard write the first letter of the verb and then a dash for each remaining letter. Give the meaning of the verb. Have students come and add the missing letter.

G _ _ _ _ _: to run like a horse

W_ _ _ : to cry

S _ _ _ _: to speak loudly

- ### Find the Best Verb

Encourage the students to find and use the most suitable verb at all times. You may call the students to the blackboard and help them replace verbs.

The frightened rabbit ran to its hole.

The verb **ran** can be replaced by

bolted hopped leaped

- ### What Do They Do?

Have the students add suitable verbs to the given nouns.

cats purr birds fly

fish _______ dogs _______

Being and Having Verbs

The word be is used as a verb. The being verbs are:
am, is, are, was, were, *be, *being, *been
***Be, being and been are only used with other verbs.**

1 Complete the sentences using **being** verbs.

am	is	are	was	were

a Hansel and Gretel _______ characters in a fairytale.

b I _______ only joking!

c She _______ twelve years old today.

d Last year they _________ too young to go by themselves.

e It _______ too cold to go for a swim today.

The words *has*, *have* and *had* are also used as verbs.

2 Underline the verbs in red.

a Where were you last night?

b The players had special jerseys to wear for the final game.

c He is a fast runner, but you are faster.

d Sarah has a new pony.

e I am upset because he is so far away.

f I once had a pet guinea pig.

g The teacher was happy because we were early.

h She has breakfast every day at 6:00 a.m.

3 Complete these sentences.

a Why were you ____?

b Have you been ____?

c She was ____.

d The players had ____.

e He has just been ____.

WORK SHEET 19

Saying Verbs

Saying verbs show how people express their feelings, for example: Sameer shouted. Ali complained. Mary mumbled. Pooja bragged.

1 Choose a verb to show how these people are expressing themselves.

promised *whispered* *growled* *complained* *shouted*

a "Hold on! I'll save you," ________________ the fireman.

b "Tania, you're always late!" ________________ the teacher.

c "Psst!" ________________ Dave. "Come and listen to this!"

d "Yes, but I always have to do it!" ________________ Kim.

e "I'll buy you a football for your birthday," Dad ________________.

2 Complete these sentences.

a Under his breath, Sumeet muttered ________________________________

____

b Patiently, Tom explained ________________________________

____

c Esha screamed, " ________________________________

____

3 How many alternative verbs for said can you think of?

____

____

____

____

____

____

____

____

____

WORK SHEET 20

Saying Verbs

Saying verbs show how people express their feelings, for example: Helen cried. Tamanna screeched. Niko shouted. Radhika moaned.

1 Choose a suitable saying verb from the word list below to complete the sentences.

NOTE: You may need to add ***–ing*** or ***–ed,*** so remember your spelling rules.

a "I can't hear you Mrs Jones," ________________ Lena.

b Someone was ________________ from the upstairs window.

c "I've lost my new lunch box," Jai ________________.

d "You'll never find out what it is!" ________________ Himani.

e "Get out of my way," ________________ the angry driver.

f "You're late again," the teacher ____________________.

g "What a wonderful surprise!" _________________ Farida.

h "You must never do that again," their mother ________________.

i "What a baby you are sometimes, Bobby," his sister _______________.

j Puneet ________________, "I always get my sums right."

Word List: Saying Verbs			
announce	*gossip*	*prattle*	*sneer*
argue	*grizzle*	*promise*	*sniffle*
ask	*growl*	*pray*	*snigger*
boast	*grumble*	*rant*	*snort*
brag	*grunt*	*rave*	*sob*
call	*hint*	*roar*	*splutter*
chat	*howl*	*say*	*stammer*
complain	*hum*	*scoff*	*stutter*
cough	*jeer*	*scold*	*talk*
cry	*laugh*	*scream*	*tease*
demand	*moan*	*shout*	*tell*
drone	*mock*	*shrug*	*wail*
exclaim	*mumble*	*sigh*	*warn*
explain	*murmur*	*sing*	*weep*
gasp	*mutter*	*skite*	*whine*
giggle	*nag*	*smile*	*whisper*

Helping Verbs

Some verbs help other verbs do their work. Together they make a verb group. Helping verbs tell us when something is happening.

am, is, are, was, were
do, did
has, have, had
shall, will
can, may, might
could, would,
should

Here are some examples:

Jasmeet ***is*** *running* to the bus.

The dog ***has*** *eaten* the bone.

I ***will*** *be driving* to Pune tomorrow.

Dad ***might*** *take* us to the zoo.

1 Circle the verb group in each sentence.

a The cat is licking its paws.

b Billy has been to Tasmania with his family.

c We can go swimming on Friday.

d Zara may be waiting for her friends at the gate.

e I will be playing cricket for the school team on Saturday.

2 Complete the verb groups.

a I am ________________ my vegetable garden.

b All the girls have been _____________ toffees.

c We were _______________ in the rock pools by the shore.

d A cow was ______________ along the track.

e They will be ______________ to school soon.

3 Colour only the helping verbs. Can you read the hidden word?

well	can	lost	has	jump	is
fly	was	see	am	come	shall
sleep	are	have	can	swim	may
run	will	read	do	look	had
eat	have	skate	might	sing	did

WORK SHEET 22

Helping Verbs

A verb is sometimes separated from its helper by another word, for example: I have often seen him here. Did you go home early?

1 Highlight the verb group in each sentence.

a It has just started to rain.

b Have you read this book yet?

c We will probably go by train.

d He is always playing computer games.

e Did they win the game of football?

A verb can be made negative by placing *not* or *never* after the helper, for example: *I do **not** want chips. They will **never** come back again. You are **not** to swim there.*

2 Complete these negative sentences.

a I do not like ______________________________

b Mum will not let me ______________________________

c Leena does not ______________________________

d The dog could not ______________________________

e Koel will not eat ______________________________

3 Rewrite the sentences in negative form.

a We will play tennis on Saturday.

____

b The pig is in its pen.

____

c They have been to the restaurant.

____

d Wait for me!

____

Verbs in Procedures

Verbs play an important part in giving instructions about how to do or make something. Most instructions are written as commands. Each instruction is introduced by a verb in the present tense.

1 Choose the correct verbs from the box to complete this recipe.

Bread and Butter pudding

INGREDIENTS:

4 slices of white bread — *2 tablespoons sugar*
1/4 cup raisins — *2 cups milk*
3 eggs — *pinch salt*

METHOD:

_______________ crusts from buttered bread.
_______________ into fingers.
_______________ the fingers in a baking dish, buttered side down, in layers.
_______________ raisins between layers.
_______________ eggs, sugar and salt together in a bowl.
_______________ milk.
_______________ until the sugar has dissolved.
_______________ over the top of the bread.
_______________ in a baking dish of hot water.
_______________ at 180° C for 40 minutes, or until custard is set.
The top should be golden brown.

stir	*cut*	*stand*	*arrange*	*add*
bake	*sprinkle*	*remove*	*beat*	*pour*

2 Write some instructions for making your favourite sandwich.

____
____
____
____
____
____

Verbs - Contractions

Many subjects and verbs are written as contractions, for example: she will = she'll I would = I'd
we have = we've they are = they're.
Usually, a pronoun subject and a helper verb contract to one word, for example: he is becomes he's.

1 Match and colour the contractions with the words they replace. Use different colours for each contraction.

I'll	they have
he's	you have
they've	I will
we're	she would
she'd	he is
you've	we are

I'm	it is
you're	we have
they're	you are
it's	he will
he'll	they are
we've	I am

I've	we will
you'll	they would
he'd	you will
she's	I have
they'd	he would
we'll	she is

NOTE: *I **should've** come with you.* should've = should **have** NOT should **of.**

2 Circle the contractions. Write the two words in full.

a I know (they've) been here before. (they have)
b It's wonderful to see you again. (__________)
c I'm sure that she'll come with us. (__________) (__________)
d We're so pleased you've arrived. (__________) (__________)
e I'd like to know why they're late. (__________) (__________)
f You'll like what he's got for you. (__________) (__________)

3 Highlight the correct word in the pair.

a (Your You're) not afraid of the dark, are you?
b (Were We're) off to the beach for holidays.
c (There They're) too old to run fast.
d I would love to see (its it's) nest.

Verbs - Contractions

Many negative verbs are written as contractions, for example: did not = didn't is not = isn't have not = haven't.

The helping verb and *not* contract into one word. An apostrophe replaces the **o** in *not*.

1 Underline the contractions. Write the words they replace in the brackets.

a She said she <u>wouldn't</u> come with me. (*would not*)

b The car hadn't been washed for weeks. (______)

c Why didn't you shut the door? (______)

d There weren't any chairs to sit on. (______)

e It isn't raining yet. (______)

2 Match and colour the contractions with the words they replace.
Use different colours for each contraction.

a doesn't	had not
b won't	were not
c hadn't	does not
d weren't	will not

e didn't	would not
f wouldn't	was not
g can't	cannot
h wasn't	did not

i haven't	do not
j aren't	have not
k don't	could not
l couldn't	are not

3 Rewrite these sentences in negative form using contractions.

a The dogs can hunt foxes. ______

b We will be going to the Easter Show. ______

c Have you seen that movie? ______

d The lawn has been mowed. ______

4 Complete the sentences.

a The sheep aren't ______

b Won't you come ______

c I just couldn't ______

WORK SHEET 26

Verbs - Subject Agreement

A simple sentence has two parts: the subject and the predicate. The verb ties the parts together.

A cheering crowd	***gathered*** along the shores of Mumbai.
SUBJECT	PREDICATE

1 Box the subject in each sentence in red.

a After dark, nocturnal animals hunt for food.

b Urick had failed in his quest to find the lost tribe of Slovia.

c The bus stopped to pick up more passengers.

d Within a month, the farmer had harvested his entire wheat crop.

e The professor peered closely at the bubbling blue liquid in the test tube.

2 Underline the verb. To find the subject, ask who or what did this. Highlight the subject.

a During the holidays, Mr and Mrs Chopra visited Tasmania.

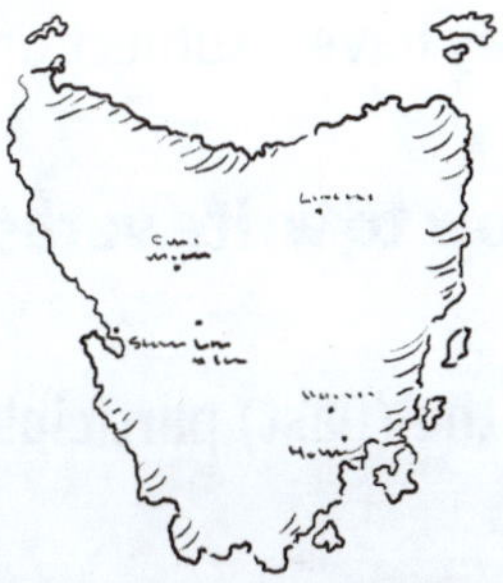

b The long and winding road led to a quaint old farmhouse.

c There are joggers down by the river.

d The children skipped through the soft carpet of fallen leaves.

e Both adults and children enjoy the rides at the fun park.

A singular subject has a singular verb, for example: The mouse ***was frightened.***
A plural subject has a plural verb, for example: The mice ***were frightened.***

3 Change the subject to plural form and rewrite the sentences.

a The climber stands at the peak of Mt Everest.

____

b The child is playing computer games.

____

c The man was watching the Grand Prix on television.

____

d A wild goose flies across the darkening sky.

____

Verb Tenses

Verbs have different tenses to show *when* things happen:

in the **present** The plane *is flying*.	in the **past** The plane *flew*.	in the **future** The plane *will fly*.

How to write verbs in the *present* tense:

- the infinitive
  - singular – He **plays** football.
  - plural – They **play** football.
- the (present) participle* with a helper
  - singular – He **is playing** football.
  - plural – They **are playing** football.

*participle: a verbal form used as an adjective. It does not specify a person or number, but may have a subject or object.

How to write verbs in the *past* tense:

- the (past) participle
  - singular – He **played** football.
  - plural – They **played** football.
- the (present) participle with a helper
  - singular – He **was playing** football.
    – He **has been playing** football.
  - plural – They **were playing** football.
    – They **have been playing** football.
- the (past) participle with a helper
  - singular – He **has played** football.
  - plural – They **have played** football.

How to write verbs in the *future* tense:

- the infinitive with the helpers *shall* and *will*
  - singular – He **will play** football.
  - plural – They **will play** football.
- *may* and *might* indicate a possible future
  - singular – He **may play** football.
  - plural - They **might play** football.
- Future tense can be shown in other ways:
  I am going to play football.
  Tomorrow, I **am playing** football.
  I **am about to play** football.

Verb Tenses

Tenses allow speakers and writers to express exactly what they want to say.

PRESENT TENSE VERBS

Tense	Number	1st person	2nd person	3rd person
Simple present	Singular	I **eat** fish	You **eat** fish.	He/she/it **eats** fish.
	Plural	We **eat** fish.	You **eat** fish.	They **eat** fish.
Present continuous	Singular	I **am eating** fish.	You **are eating** fish.	He/she/it **is eating** fish.
	Plural	We **are eating** fish.	You **are eating** fish.	They **are eating** fish.
Present perfect	Singular	I **have eaten** fish.	You **have eaten** fish.	He/she/it **has eaten** fish.
	Plural	We **have eaten** fish.	You **have eaten** fish.	They **have eaten** fish.
Perfect continuous	Singular	I **have been eating** fish.	You **have been eating** fish.	He/she/it **has been eating** fish.
	Plural	We **have been eating** fish.	You **have been eating** fish.	They **have been eating** fish.

PAST TENSE VERBS

Tense	Number	1st person	2nd person	3rd person
Simple past	Singular	I **ate** fish	You **ate** fish.	He/she/it **ate** fish.
	Plural	We **ate** fish.	You **ate** fish.	They **ate** fish.
Past continuous	Singular	I **was eating** fish.	You **were eating** fish.	He/she/it **was eating** fish.
	Plural	We **were eating** fish.	You **were eating** fish.	They **were eating** fish.
Past perfect	Singular	I **had eaten** fish.	You **had eaten** fish.	He/she/it **had eaten** fish.
	Plural	We **had eaten** fish.	You **had eaten** fish.	They **had eaten** fish.
Perfect continuous	Singular	I **had been eating** fish.	You **had been eating** fish.	He/she/it **had been eating** fish.
	Plural	We **had been eating** fish.	You **had been eating** fish.	They **had been eating** fish.

FUTURE TENSE VERBS

Tense	Number	1st person	2nd person	3rd person
Simple future	Singular	I **will eat** fish	You **will eat** fish.	He/she/it **will eat** fish.
	Plural	We **will eat** fish.	You **will eat** fish.	They **will eat** fish.
Future continuous	Singular	I **will be eating** fish.	You **will be eating** fish.	He/she/it **will be eating** fish.
	Plural	We **will be eating** fish.	You **will be eating** fish.	They **will be eating** fish.
Future perfect	Singular	I **will have eaten** fish.	You **will have eaten** fish.	He/she/it **will have eaten** fish.
	Plural	We **will have eaten** fish.	You **will have eaten** fish.	They **will have eaten** fish.
Future perfect continuous	Singular	I **will have been eating** fish.	You **will have been eating** fish.	He/she/it **will have been eating** fish.
	Plural	We **will have been eating** fish.	You **will have been eating** fish.	They **will have been eating** fish.

We can even add other verbs to clarify our meaning, for example:

*I **could** have been eating fish. They **should** be eating fish. He **might** have eaten fish. We **can** eat fish.*

Verb Tenses

Read the following sentences and notice the different forms of the verb **walk.**

I walk everyday. : simple present
I am walking now. : present continuous
I walked yesterday. : simple past
I was walking yesterday. : past continuous
I will walk tomorrow. : simple future
I will be walking tomorrow. : future continuous

Forms of verbs

Another way that we can write the forms of verbs is as follows.

Base	-s, -es or -ies	-ing	past
go	goes	going	went
cry	cries	crying	cried
eat	eats	eating	ate

Continuous tenses

-ing words are used to describe actions that are going on in the present, were going on in the past or will be going on in the future.

The **present continuous** describes an action that is happening at the present moment. It has already begun but the action has not ended. The verb group uses words like **am, is, are.**

For example: I am going. They are leaving.

The **past continuous** shows an action that was going on in the past or when something happened suddenly. This verb group is used with words such as **while, when, as.**

For example: When their mother came home, they were having lunch.

The children started eating before their mother came and were still eating when she entered the house.

The **future continuous** tense is used for an action that will be going on at a time in future.

Verb Tenses

Look at the picture below.

This picture shows that the boys are planning to go somewhere the following day and one of them has agreed to wait for the other one. **Shall be waiting** is the future continuous of **wait.**

Past participle and Perfect tenses

A past participle indicates past or completed action. It is formed by adding **-d** or **-ed** to the base form of regular verbs.

Look at the table below.

Base form	Past tense form	Past participle form
Want	Wanted	Wanted
Eat	Ate	Eaten
Hide	Hid	Hidden
Begin	Began	Begun
See	Saw	Seen
Sow	Sowed	Sown
Take	Took	Taken
Kneel	Knelt	Knelt
Go	Went	Gone
Drive	Drove	Driven

In many cases the past participle form is the same as the simple past tense form.

Past participles end with **–d**, **-ed**, **-n**, **-en**, **-t.**

Verb Tenses

Games

- ### Change When it Happened

Divide the class into two teams. Give a sentence to Team A and Team B will change the sentence and say it in past tense. You can revise all the tenses and their continuous forms in this activity.

- ### Rewrite the News

Give the students copies of a news article. Ask them to rewrite the article in present tense.

Verb Tenses

Verbs tell us when things are happening: in the present in the past or in the future.

1 Fill in the missing verb from these present tense happenings and then draw them.

SINGULAR	The sun ____ shining.	A helicopter ____ hovering.	Someone ____ knocking.
PLURAL	The balls ____ bouncing.	We ____ reading.	They ____ skateboarding.

2 Add a verb or verb group in the past tense.

a The skydiver ____________________ to the ground.

b The mountaineer ____________________ the high alpine peaks.

c He ____________________ a taxi and ____________________ to the train station.

d The athletes ____________________ flags for the final march-past.

e Fearlessly, he ____________________ beneath the waves.

3 Write the past tense of these verbs.

**Spelling alert!*

Regular past tense is formed by adding *–ed*.

a gather ____________	*f* stumble ____________	*k* throb ____________
b float ____________	*g* untie ____________	*l* scan ____________
c unlock ____________	*h* receive ____________	*m* hum ____________
d display ____________	*i* score ____________	*n* grin ____________
e wander ____________	*j* invite ____________	*o* spot ____________

Verb Tenses

Some past tense verbs are irregular in their spelling. They are not formed by adding -ed to the infinitive.

1 Complete this table of common past tense verbs.

a eat ________	*e* is ________	*i* run ________
b give ________	*f* sing ________	*j* has ________
c come ________	*g* grow ________	*k* stand ________
d dig ________	*h* do ________	*l* break ________

2 Change the present tense verb (underlined) to past tense.

a We <u>buy</u> eggs. <u>bought</u>

b I <u>light</u> a candle. ________

c He <u>sees</u> a crow. ________

d They <u>sit</u> on chairs. ________

e She <u>keeps</u> a cow. ________

f We <u>spend</u> money. ________

g He <u>goes</u> home. ________

h I <u>catch</u> a ball. ________

i He <u>throws</u> darts. ________

j We <u>go</u> to school. ________

3 Write sentences to say what you think you will be doing:

a tomorrow ***b*** next week ***c*** this evening
d at lunch time ***e*** when you grow up

a ________________________________

b ________________________________

c ________________________________

d ________________________________

e ________________________________

Go back and highlight your verb groups. These verbs show FUTURE tense.

Verb Tenses

We use –ing when an action is going on. Such words are verbs. At times, however, an –ing word becomes an adjective. It describes a noun.
For example: burning train, barking dog

1 Look at the pictures and write appropriate **–ing** words to describe them.

____________________ ____________________ ____________________

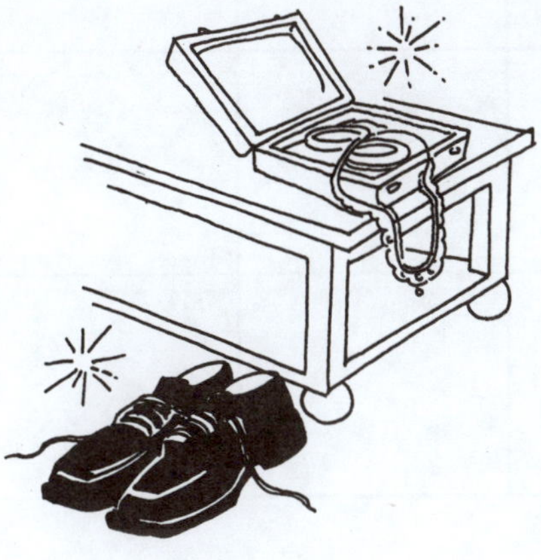

____________________ ____________________ ____________________

Verb Tenses

Some past tense verbs are irregular in their spelling. They are not formed by adding -ed to the infinitive.

1 Complete the following table.

The first row is done for you.

Everyday (Simple present)	Now (Present continuous)	Yesterday (Simple past)	Was (Past continuous)	Simple future	Will be (Future continuous)
I stand.	I am standing.	I stood.	I was standing.	I will stand.	I will be standing.
You catch					
I see					
I cut					
I do					

Verb Tenses

Verbs tell us when things are happening: in the present in the past or in the future. Continuous tenses describe actions that are happening.

1 Fill in the correct form of the verbs given in brackets.

a The price of many items has ______________ (go) up.

b He ____________ (shake) the bottle before he _____________ (take) out the medicine.

c The lion ____________ (spring) at the jungle guard.

d When the clock ____________ (strike) one, the mouse ____________ (run) down.

e I ____________ (buy) this dress last year.

f Miss Ravina _____________ (teach) us English.

g The trees have ______________ (grow) taller than last year.

h He ___________ (read) a book before he ____________ (go) to bed every night.

2 Fill in the blanks with the present continuous form of the verb given in brackets.

a He _____________ the cupboard this evening. (clean)

b Mummy _____________ a cake for us. (bake)

c Do not disturb him. He is _____________ his homework. (complete)

d She said she is _______________ some books tonight. (bring)

e They were ______________ up the tree to pluck some mangoes. (climb)

3 Fill in the blanks with the past continuous forms of the verbs given in brackets.

a They ________________ when I knocked at the door. (sleep)

b As he _______________ the plants, it began to rain. (water)

c While she _____________ the shelves, he ______________ the floor. (dust, sweep)

d While you _____________, he broke the vase. (not look)

e He jumped off the bus while it was ______________. (still move)

Verb Tenses

The present continuous tense describes an action that is happening at the present moment. The past continuous tense describes an action that was going on in the past. The future continuous tense describes an action that will happen in the future.

1 Fill in the blanks with the future continuous tense of the verb in the brackets.

a You ______ to school at 8 o'clock tomorrow morning. (go)

b The men ________ the road whole of next week. (repair)

c They ________ with cold when they come out of the icy cold water. (shiver)

d By the time they arrive, we _______ dressed. (get)

e I _______ you in half an hour's time. (call)

2 Rewrite the following passage in future continuous tense.

A young man inherited a great fortune after the death of his father. The lure of riches meant little to him. His heart was filled with the love of God. He set out to identify someone who would guide him to find the truth. He found such a teacher. He stayed with the teacher. He sold all that he had and became his disciple.

____

____

____

____

____

____

____

Revision 1

1 Look at the pictures in the two columns and make compound nouns.

A	
drum	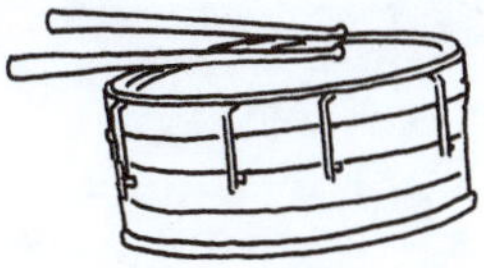
letter	
tooth	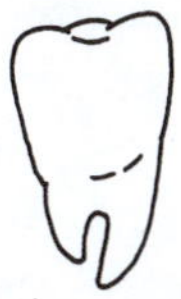
book	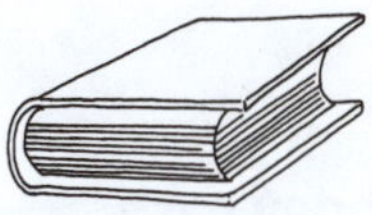

B	
box	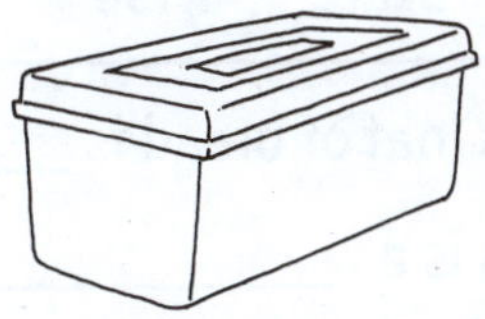
shelf	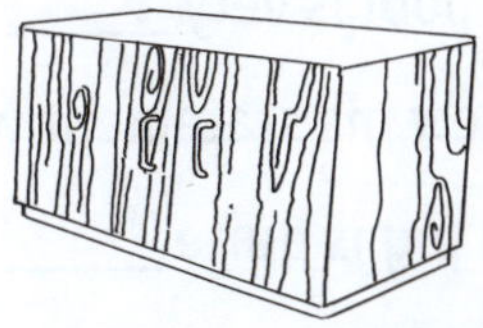
stick	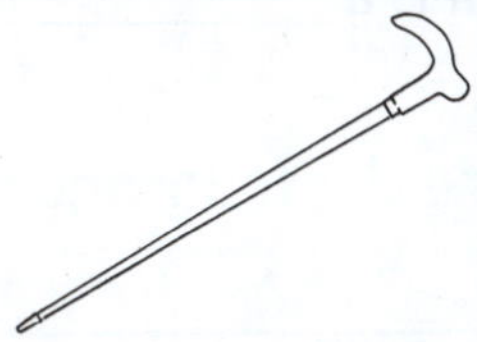
brush	

2 Complete the following phrases.

a A troop of __________

b A __________ of fish

c A __________ of cattle

d A bunch of __________

3 Write the abstract noun of the following adjectives.

a happy __________

b wise __________

c confident __________

d brave __________

4 Choose the adjective from the box that has the opposite meaning to the adjective in the brackets.

thin	stale	wise	safe	shallow	false

a This loaf of bread is ________________. (fresh)

b This is a ________________ spot to swim. (dangerous)

c The pool is very ________________ here. (deep)

d I knew his statement was ________________. (true)

e This pig is quite ________________. (plump)

f Tom is a ________________ boy. (foolish)

5 Complete the following sentences with the correct verbs.

a I ________________ trying to play the piano.

b They ________________ too old to play cricket.

c She ________________ shouting in my ears.

d I ________________ my friend that I would attend her birthday party.

e I once ________________ a pet tortoise.

f An announcement ________________ made by the principal.

g I ________________ be going to my village tomorrow.

h We ________________ see a movie next Tuesday.

i ________________ you drive?

j ________________ I see your photo album?

6 Complete the table to show the forms of verbs.
The first one is done for you.

eat	eats	eating	ate
love			
go			
scream			
buy			
do			

Revision 1

7 Rewrite the following sentences in the simple past and simple future tense.

a The sun shines brightly.

____

b The koel sings sweetly.

____

c She throws the ball.

____

8 Identify the continuous tenses in the following sentences.

a The old man will be slowly climbing up the stairs. ______________

b The moon is giving out light. ______________

c Ram was staying in a hotel. ______________

d They were telling a story. ______________

9 Write the past tense and the past participle form of the following verbs.

One row has been done for you.

Base form	Past tense	Past participle
take	took	taken
ride		
laugh		
begin		
forget		

Revision 1

10 Rewrite the following sentences keeping the subject-verb agreement in mind.

a His mother always bake cakes.

____

b He should writes to us.

____

c Captains of the ship spreads the map in front when sailing.

____

d Our books is on the shelf.

____

e They wait for we at the bus stop.

____

f The sun rise above the hills.

____

11 Read the following passage and answer the questions.

"Let's go or it will be time for lunch before we know it," said Meena. As always they had come to Bishnupur for a vacation with their grandparents. It was a small, quiet town surrounded by green hills and some ancient ruins. They loved going for walks and spent hours exploring the old temple in a fort nearby. At times, they pretended to be rulers of an ancient kingdom.

a Write the full form of let's _______________

b Give another word for vacation _______________

c Give two words that describe Bishnupur _______________ _______________

d Which word has the same meaning as ancient _______________

e Where was the old fort situated?

____

f What did Meena and her brother like to do?

____

12 Imagine that you are a king/queen. How would you rule your kingdom? Write five sentences.

Articles

A, an and the are three articles. A and an are indefinite articles and the is a definite article.

Three articles—**a**, **an**, **the**—are used to signal nouns or noun groups.

a	**an**	**the**

- **A** and **an** are only used with **singular** nouns. They are **indefinite** because they point to something that is not known by the reader or the listener.
- **A** is used before a word beginning with a **consonant**, for example: a rose, a computer, a clever girl.
- **An** is used before a word beginning with a **vowel**, for example: an orange, an odd person, an igloo.
- **An** is also used before a word beginning with an '**h**' (not sounded), for example: an hour, an honest man.
- **The** is a **definite** article because it points to something that has been made known to the reader or listener, for example: the cap I wear, the ball in the box.
- **The** is always used before **plural** nouns, for example: the eggs in the nest, the children at school.
- **The** is also used when it points to a common noun known by everyone, for example: the sun, the morning.

NOTE: A character in a story is usually introduced as **a**. (For example: There was once **a** giant, **a** red fox, **a** beautiful princess, **a** brave knight ...)

Once the character has been introduced, they can be referred to as **the**. (For example: **The** giant spoke ..., **The** red fox prowled ..., **The** princess lived ...)

Articles

A, an and the are called articles.

Rules for using a, an and the

A is used:

- Before a word beginning with a consonant.
- Before vowels which have the sound **yu**.
  For example: a union, a university, a unit
- Before the word one.
  For example: a one-way street

An is used:

- Before words beginning with a vowel.
  For example, an egg, an umbrella
- Before a word beginning with a silent h.
  For example, an heir, an honest man

The is used:

- To refer to a particular person or thing.
  For example: the naughty boy, the big house
- With names of rivers, oceans, gulfs, mountain ranges, islands.
  For example: the Yamuna, the Andaman and Nicobar Islands
- When sacred books or newspapers are spoken of.
  For example, the Gita, the Bible, the *Indian Express*
- When we refer to directions.
  For example: the east
- When we refer to races and certain regions or nations.
  For example: the Deccan, the United States of America
- When the words kingdom, republic, state, etc. precede the name of any country.
  For example, the Republic of India
- For offices or titles.
  For example: the President of India, the King of England, the Dalai Lama

Articles

The is not used:

- For names of town or cities.
- To refer to countries except the ones discussed above.
- For names of mountain peaks.
  For example: Mount Everest
- For names of historical figures.
  For example: Netaji, Akbar
- For names of streets.
  For example: Mahatama Gandhi Road, Hanuman Lane
- For the days of the week or months of the year.
- For names of precious metals, material.

Games

- **Writing without Articles**
  Allow the students to write their own paragraphs or short stories leaving out the articles the, a and an. They can then give the puzzles to their classmates to solve.

- **Change the Article**
  Ask the students to change an indefinite article to the definite article by adding descriptive words.
  I saw a cat.
  I saw the big, black cat.

- **Spot the Articles**
  Give the students copies of newspaper or magazine articles. They can read the text and spot the articles.

WORK SHEET 33

Articles

A and an are indefinite articles. The is a definite article.

1 Write words that will go with the following articles.

An ____________ A ____________

An ____________ A ____________

An ____________ A ____________

The ____________ The ____________

2 Fill in the blanks with a, an, the or x (nothing).

a ____ George Scot has four sons. He named all of his sons ____ George. The kids at school often tease ____ Georges.

b Does ____ teacher in your History class use computers?

c Two years ago, Mary bought ____ laptop computer. ____ computer is not very good, because it breaks often. Last night, ____ laptop broke again. Mary became so angry that she threw ____ machine away.

d Please meet me at the station in _____ hour from now.

e I like to watch tennis on television. It is ____ very good sport.

f My brother won a medal for being ______ best runner in school.

g Please bring _____ oranges from the table.

h I couldn't believe my eyes when I saw ______ elephant crossing the road in front of my house yesterday.

i How much will it cost to go on ______ holiday to Spain?

j ______ President of India will be visiting Australia next week.

Adverbs

Adverbs are words that give more meaning to:

- a **verb** (He runs fast.)
- an **adjective** (He is a very fast runner.)
- another **adverb** (He runs too fast for me.)

Adverbs tell us how, when and where things happen.
It is easy to spot the adverb — they add meaning to verbs, adjectives and other adverbs, NEVER to nouns.

Read the following sentences.
She writes neatly.
She walked fast.
The word neatly describes how she writes and fast describes how she walks.

Adverbs of manner

The **–ly** adverbs are adverbs that show how an action is done. They are known as adverbs of manner.
For example: He nodded anxiously.
She spoke slowly.

Adverbs of time

These adverbs tell when things happen.
For example: yesterday, tomorrow, long ago, next week, on Tuesday, now
Adverbs of time also tell how often things happen.
For example: often, usually, once, twice, daily

Adverbs of place

These adverbs tell where things are happening.
For example: here, there, somewhere, around, over, away

Adverbs of degree

These adverbs show the extent to which something happens.
For example: very, almost, nearly, completely

Adverbs

Adverbs, like adjectives, also have three forms:

- Positive degree: He shouted loudly.
- Comparative degree: He shouted more loudly still.
- Superlative degree: He shouted most loudly of all.

Generally, we add **–er** or **–est** to adverbs of one syllable.
For example: high, higher, highest; hard, harder, hardest
Thus, some adverbs will look like adjectives.
Remember that adverbs add meaning to verbs, adjectives and other adverbs NEVER to nouns.

Adverbs ending in **–ly** have **more** or **most** before them.
For example: silently, more silently, most silently
Some adverbs of degree are irregular.
For example: well, better, best; much, more, most; badly, worse, worst

Games

- ### Make the Right Choice

  Ask the students to list suitable adverbs to complete a sentence.
  I can walk ...

  quickly lazily proudly slowly

- ### Replacing Words

  Divide the class into two teams. Let the members of one team provide a group of words and the members of the other team provide one word to replace the group of words.
  The tortoise walks in a **slow manner.**
  The tortoise walks **slowly.**

Adverbs - Intensify and Modify

Adverbs add meaning to adjectives and other adverbs. These adverbs modify or intensify the meaning, for example:

extremely fit very old	fairly slow nearly there
(intensifiers)	**(modifiers)**

1 Complete the sentences with adverbs from the box. Compare your answers with others. Note how the choice of adverb modifies or intensifies the meaning.

a The building was constructed from ________________ new materials.

b We were not ________________ concerned about the results of the match.

c I am ________________ puzzled by your answer.

d The journey was ________________ long and ________________ tiring.

e He was ________________ worried about the situation on the island.

f She was feeling ________________ lonely and ________________ unhappy.

g We know they are ________________ slow creatures.

h I am not ________________ sure they are telling the truth.

entirely	*very*	*too*	*overly*	*quite*	*fairly*
deeply	*somewhat*	*extremely*	*rather*	*absolutely*	*really*

2 Write sentences with these modified adjectives.

quite long *rather silly* *almost ripe*

____

____

____

3 Write sentences with these intensified adjectives.

incredibly bright *extremely fast* *deeply troubled*

____

____

____

Adverbs - Manner, Time, Place

Adverbs add meaning to verbs, adjectives and other adverbs, for example:
She runs fast. She is a very fast runner.
She runs too fast for me.

There are three types of adverbs that say more about verbs.

1 **MANNER** – tells *how* an action occurs.
2 **TIME** – tells *when* an action occurs.
3 **PLACE** – tells *where* an action occurs.

1 The adverb in each sentence is underlined. Does it say HOW or WHEN or WHERE about the verb?

a Small birds <u>often</u> come to drink in our bird bath. ________
b I couldn't find my car keys <u>anywhere</u>. ________
c <u>Tomorrow</u> we are going to visit the historical museum. ________
d She spoke <u>hesitantly</u>, as if she didn't know what to say. ________
e Sit <u>here</u> and wait till I come back. ________
f Dad was <u>pleasantly</u> surprised when he opened his gift. ________

2 Highlight the adverbs in each sentence. Remember adverbs tell HOW, WHEN and WHERE.

a Donna is catching a train early this morning.
b He tapped his fingers impatiently on the table.
c I will stay here with all my friends.
d The farmers looked anxiously at the dark storm clouds.
e I seldom see my cousin since she left our town.
f Sometimes my brother and I go cycling.
g The man always drives carefully.

3 Use these adverbs in sentences: *everywhere, occasionally, kindly.*

____

____

____

Adverbs - Manner, Time, Place

Adverbs add meaning to verbs. They tell us how, when and where things happen.

1 Add an adverb from those listed below.

a The couple waltzed ________________ round the dance floor. (how)

b ____________ I went to the science museum. (when)

c The students worked _________ on their clay models. (how)

d We ______________ go skiing in winter. (when)

e Tiny crabs scuttled sideways __________ the sand. (where)

f The helicopter lifted _________ into the air. (where)

upwards	*once*	*yesterday*	*sideways*
sometimes	*gracefully*	*often*	*busily*

2 The adverbs have been underlined. Draw an arrow from the adverb to the verb it tells more about. Do the adverbs say HOW, WHEN or WHERE about the verb?

a Aditya called <u>excitedly</u> to his friends. *how*

b <u>Occasionally</u> we go swimming in the creek. ________

c If you arrive <u>late</u>, you may not get a seat. ________

d Sit <u>there</u> and read your book <u>quietly</u>. ________ ________

e Autumn leaves fell <u>down</u> on the soft ground. ________

f Our cousins arrived from Sweden <u>yesterday</u>. ________

3 Write sentences using the adverbs: *homewards, tomorrow, sadly.*

____

____

____

Adverbs showing Degree

Adverbs need to be placed correctly in a sentence, or they can change or confuse the meaning.
These adverbs are often misplaced: only, just, also, almost, even, mainly. **These adverbs should be placed before the words they modify.**

1 Place a ^ where you think the adverbs should go. Now see if the adverbs can be placed at another place in the sentence. Note any differences in meaning.

a Radha gave Raman three dollars. (only)
b He got home as the sun went down. (just)
c Mallika was told to rewrite her report. (also)
d It was Aditya who was to blame. (mainly)
e Anita thought she saw a falling star. (even)

2 Write sentences using: ***just, only, also.***

____

____

____

Like adjectives, adverbs show degree. And like adjectives, many are formed by adding *-er* **and** *-est*. **Adverbs ending in** *-ly* **need** *more* **or** *most*, **for example:**
soon sooner soonest *evenly more evenly most evenly*

3 Colour the matching adverbs of degree.

Adverb	Comparative	Superlative
late	harder	highest
early	further	hardest
high	later	earliest
hard	higher	farthest
far	earlier	latest

4 Complete the table using *more* and *most*.

Adverb	Comparative	Superlative
easily	more easily	most easily
often		
carefully		
eagerly		
happily		

Adverbs Showing Degree

Adverbs have three forms—positive, comparative and superlative.

1 Fill in the blanks using the correct adverb.

a This orange tastes _______ than that one. (better, best)

b The red car travels _______. Does the blue car go _________? Of the red, blue and green car which travels the ________? (faster, fastest, fast)

c A lion eats ______ than a cat. (most, more)

d Of all the children Raman sang the _______. (loud, loudest)

e Bob jumps ______ than Josh. (higher, high)

f You have spoilt my _______ shirt. (better, best)

g I hope Jay will try ________ the next time. (harder, hard)

2 Rewrite the following sentences using the adverb in the bracket in its correct place.

One has been done for you.

a I have read that book before. (never)
I have never read that book before.

b We visit him on Sundays. (sometimes)

____

c She is late for work. (rarely)

____

d Yes, I do. (usually)

____

e I am at home in the mornings. (generally)

____

f I go to the library on the weekend. (always)

____

g Have you visited New York? (ever)

____

Pronouns

Pronouns are words used in place of nouns.
For example: I, me, you, your, he, she
These are also known as **personal pronouns.** They are used to refer to ourselves, people we are talking to and people whom we are talking about. We can thus refer to three persons—one who is talking, the person to whom we speak and the person about whom we speak.

For example: "I told you I will not hire Ravi because he is a lazy person," Rohit told Harry.
Rohit is the speaker. The pronoun used is **I** (first-person pronoun).
Harry is the person spoken to. The pronoun used is **you** (second-person pronoun).
Ravi is the person spoken about. The pronoun used is **he** (third-person pronoun).

Look at the table to understand personal pronouns.

Person	Singular	Plural
First	I, me, my, mine	we, us, our, ours
Second	you, yours	you (your), yours
Third	Common: it (its) Masculine: he, him (his) Feminine: she, her (hers)	they, them, their(theirs)

Possessive pronouns show belongingness.
For example: hers, theirs
The words in brackets in the table are possessive adjectives.
For example: his chair, their books
Interrogative pronouns are used to ask certain questions — Who? Whom? Whose? Which? What?
For example: Who ate all the cookies?
Whom did you see?
Whose books are on the floor?
Which bus did you take?
What is your address?

Pronouns

Games

- ### Pick and Paste

  Write a passage on the blackboard, leaving spaces for the pronouns. Write the missing pronouns on small chits and keep them in a bowl on the table. Ask the students to pick up a slip each and stick the correct pronoun on the board.

- ### Buzz for a Pronoun

  Read aloud a short passage. Ask the students to shout out 'Buzz' when they hear a pronoun. Points can be awarded for correctly identifying the pronouns.

Pronouns

Personal pronouns replace the names of the people, places, animals and everyday things around us.

1 Underline the personal pronouns in the following sentences. (First person in green, second person in blue and third person in red)

a He was told not to tease the dog but he did not listen to me and it snapped at him.

b You should speak to him gently for he is a child.

c They told us that they have a holiday today and they will not go to school.

d When do you think they will tell them what they have done?

e You were out so I told them that they could not meet you.

f We asked our father if we could invite them for a movie.

2 Fill in the blanks with suitable personal pronouns.

a ______ have to meet ______ friend and cannot come to ______ house.

b ______ are going for a picnic.

c Our teacher told ______ that ______ could not leave the class till ______ finished ______ work.

d Can ______ please complete this task for ______? ______ am not sure how to do it.

e ______ can go for the party with ______.

f ______ parents were looking for ______. Where did ______ go after school?

g Is that __________ car?

Interrogative Pronouns

Some pronouns are used to ask questions, such as: Who? Which? What? Whose? Whom?

1 Answer these questions.

a What do you like for breakfast? ____________________

b Who is your best friend? ____________________

c Whose house is next door to yours? ____________________

d Which TV show do you like best? ____________________

2 Now it's your turn. Write four questions and ask a friend to answer them.

a Who ____________________?

____

b Which ____________________?

____

c What ____________________?

____

d Whose ____________________?

____

3 Unscramble these questions. Remember to use question marks.

a gold lost a Who watch ____________________

b socks lying the are floor Whose on ____________________

c book What you reading are ____________________

d in with Who playing park the was you ____________________

e is to river it Which way the ____________________

4 Fill in the missing pronouns in these sentences.

a ________ is Dad doing in the shed?

b ________ was that masked man?

c ________ flavour do you like best—chocolate or vanilla?

d ________ dog is that running down the street?

e To ________ it may concern.

Revision 2

1 Read the sentences below. Mention whether the underlined words are adjectives or adverbs and what kind are they.

a She drives carefully and has not had a single accident.

_______ _______

b Look at the lovely girl walking round and round the bush.

_______ _______

c The furry dog was sitting comfortably below that chair.

_______ _______

d A huge crowd had collected to witness the second match yesterday.

____

e That new house was purchased by Mina last month.

_______ _______ _______

2 Match the following verbal adjectives to the nouns they describe.

a	Cooked	river
b	Flowing	dog
c	Falling	dish
d	Spotted	book
e	Barking	leopard
f	Exciting	leaves

3 Rewrite the sentences correctly.

Jane is the best of the two sisters.

____

He is the short of all the people at the party.

____

He got the less marks in the class.

____

Sheena can walk fast than Meena.

____

Revision 2

4 In the table given below write the comparative degrees of the adverbs and adjectives.

Positive	Comparative	Superlative
thin		
wet		
old		
soft		
easily		
often		
neatly		
early		

5 Arrange the words to form questions.

a socks whose lost are

____

b is river way which the to

____

c are doing what you

____

d is house yours to the which next

____

6 Frame questions using the following question words.

a Who ______________________________

b What ______________________________

c Which ______________________________

7 Use pronouns where necessary in the following paragraph.

My friend Rita is a sweet girl. Rita loves to eat chocolates. Rita has a dog called Ruffles. Rita and Ruffles visit Mita often. Rita, Ruffles and Mita play in the garden. Rita, Ruffles and Mita enjoy themselves.

Prepositions

A preposition is a word that shows the relationship between a noun or pronoun used with it and some other word in the sentence. It is used to show position, direction or time.

Remember:

- A preposition usually comes before a noun or pronoun.
  For example: The apples are kept on the table.
- The noun or pronoun that follows a preposition is called the object of the preposition.
  For example: John sat beside the pool.
- Generally, a preposition comes before its object, but sometimes it can follow its object. This often occurs in questions.
  For example: Which country are you from?

behind

beside

between

in

in front

on

over

under

Problem prepositions

Among/Between

Something is shared among three or more people. Something is shared between two people.

I shared the cake **among** the entire class.

I shared the cake **between** mummy and myself.

In/Into

In shows position in one place. Into shows movement from one place to another.

The milk is **in** the jug.

The girl dived **into** the pool.

Prepositions

Different from

One thing or person is always different **from** another. Never use different **than.**

Beside/Besides

Beside means at the side of. Besides means in addition to.
Raman stood **beside** the bed.
Several ladies were there **besides** Mary.

Games

- ### Using Place Words

  Display a large poster or a picture. Have the students explain the positions of certain objects in the picture.

- ### Instructions for You

  Let the students work in pairs. One student can give instructions to his/her partner. The partner then carries out the instructions.
  Go to the class. Pick up a piece of chalk. Draw a cat on the blackboard.

- ### Where Is It?

  Ask the students to describe the position of some objects in the classroom.
  Where is the pile of books? On the table
  Where is the dustbin? Under the table
  Where are the clips? In the cupboard

Prepositions

Prepositions usually come before a noun or a pronoun.

1 Fill in the blanks with the correct prepositions.

a Have you seen a horse ______ a tail?

b I received a letter ________ my grandma.

c Don't lean _____ the wall.

d He kicked the ball _____ the window.

e The child is doing the project _____ himself.

f What is he talking ______?

g The cow jumped ______ the fence.

h The bottle is full ______ water.

i Let's sit here and wait _____ mom.

j The man slowly crossed the hot desert _______ his camel

2 Use the following prepositions in sentences of your own.

at ____________________

upon ____________________

beside ____________________

with ____________________

Conjunctions

Conjunctions are words that link or join two or more words or a group of words or sentences. They are also called joining words.

For example: and, but, or, until, because, since, though, nor, for, so

Rita **and** Mohan are in school. (joining two words)

Sunil caught me **but** I ran away. (joining two sentences)

Some conjunctions are also used in pairs.

either ... or

For example: We could **either** go to the library **or** sit in the park.

neither ... nor

For example: **Neither** did he finish his homework **nor** did he study for the test.

both ... and

For example: **Both** Soma **and** Suresh were invited to the party.

whether ... or

For example: Have you decided **whether** you will go **or** not?

not only ... but also

For example: Tanya is **not only** clever, **but also** hard-working.

no sooner ... than

For example: **No sooner** had I reached the road, **than** the bus came.

so that

For example: I am saving money **so that** I can buy a car.

Conjunctions

Words such as and, but, or, since, because, nor, for and so are used to join sentences.

1 Join the following sentences with appropriate conjunctions.

a It is very hot. You can't drink it now.

___

b He was talking softly. We could not hear him.

___

c She opened the door. She let us in.

___

d Hurry up. We will go without you.

___

e Milk is tasty. Milk is nutritious.

___

2 Choose the correct conjunction to fill in the blanks.

a I would like to go, ___ I do not have a car. (but, nor)

b He has not written, ___ has he called me. (but, nor)

c Dad opened the window ___ looked out. (and, yet)

d Rama was not in the backyard, ___ was she upstairs. (or, nor)

e The sun had set, ___ it was still bright outside. (or, yet)

f Do you know Mohan's address ___ telephone number? (but, or)

g My brother has not arrived yet, ___ have they. (and, nor)

h Sonia read the book, ___ did not understand it. (but, or)

i I went for a walk ___ the sun was shining. (because, otherwise)

j Mr Patel invited him ___ his friends. (and, but)

k Johny can't carry the bucket ___ it is too heavy (so, because)

Sentences

A sentence is a group of words that make sense. A sentence must at least have one verb. A sentence begins with a capital letter and ends with a full stop, question or exclamation mark.

Simple sentences have two parts — a subject and a predicate, which contains the verb.

Little Bo-Peep	lost her sheep.
subject	predicate (with the verb)

Bobby	climbed the tree.
subject	predicate (with the verb)

There are four types of sentences:
A **declarative or assertive** sentence states facts or opinions. It starts with a capital letter and ends with a full stop.
For example: He is a clever boy.
It is windy today.

An **imperative** sentence is one that makes a request or gives an order. Such sentences begin with a capital letter and end with a full stop. Commands usually begin with a verb in the present tense.
For example: Come here.
Kindly hear me out.

An **interrogative** sentence asks questions. It begins with a capital letter and ends with a question mark.
For example: Is she coming today?
Where are you going?

An **exclamatory** sentence is one that expresses some strong emotion or feeling. It begins with a capital letter and ends with an exclamation mark.
For example: What a wonderful play!

Sentences

Interjections are single words/incomplete sentences that express feelings and emotions.

For example: Wow!

How lovely!

Goodness me!

We use exclamation marks after an interjection.

Speech marks are used around spoken words in dialogue.

For example: "Dinner at seven o'clock," called Mum.

"What are we having?" Jose replied.

A sentence with **no** or **not** is a **negative sentence.** A sentence without a **no** or **not** is a **positive sentence.** A positive sentence is also called an **affirmative** or **declaratory** sentence.

Examples of negative sentences are: He is not short.

The parrots are not sitting on the tree.

Game

- **Telephone Conversation**

  Ask the students to work in pairs. One student says a positive sentence, the other one says the same sentence in a negative manner. The second student then says a positive sentence and the first one says the same in a negative manner.

Sentences - Subject and Predicate

Simple sentences have two parts. The subject is tied to the rest of the sentence or predicate by a verb.

1 Write four more sentences about the same subject.

The old yellow bus is travelling along the dusty road.

a ______________________________

b ______________________________

c ______________________________

d ______________________________

2 Add a subject so that each sentence makes sense.

a ____________________ put ten rupees in her piggy bank.

b Up the steep hill went ____________________.

c At the bottom of the hole ____________________.

d ____________________ escaped into the forest.

e ____________________ lost his map and compass.

3 Write a predicate for each of these sentences that describe the picture.

a The young man ____________________.

b The umbrella ____________________.

c The water ____________________.

d A glass of lemonade ____________________.

Types of sentences

A declarative sentence states facts. An imperative sentence makes a request or gives an order. An interrogative sentence asks questions. An exclamatory sentence expresses some strong feeling.

1 What kind of sentences are the following? Write D for declarative, IN for interrogative, IM for imperative and E for exclamatory sentences.

a What a terrible mistake! __________

b Meet me in the market. __________

c Have I made a mistake? __________

d The grass has been cut. __________

e That is a beautiful dress! __________

f Do not leave the room. __________

g Can she do it by herself? __________

h She has fever. __________

i What did you see? __________

j Please give me your book. __________

2 Frame questions for the following sentences.

a She is going to the market.

____

b I like that dress the most.

____

c The ship sailed for the Andamans.

____

d My friends are coming here in the evening.

____

e We will visit my uncle next week.

____

Affirmative and Negative Sentences

Positive sentences are called affirmative sentences. Negative sentences have no or not in them.

1 Rewrite the following sentences as negative.

a They have heard the news.

____

b The shop is open.

____

c They have arrived already.

____

d He will show you the way.

____

e Kate bought some flowers.

____

f We lost the game last evening.

____

g The girl fed the cat.

____

h We left school at one o' clock.

____

Sentences – Exclamations

Some sentences show sudden surprise, delight or horror. They are called exclamations. They begin with a capital letter and end in an exclamation mark, for example: Stop! Help! No way! What! Late again! Get out!

1 Complete each sentence with a full stop or an exclamation mark. Justify your reasons.

a I went to the pet shop to buy a white rabbit ______________

b You left it on the bus ______________

c Man overboard ______________

d Let's play cricket in the backyard ______________

e What a wonderful party ______________

2 Write an exclamation for each picture.

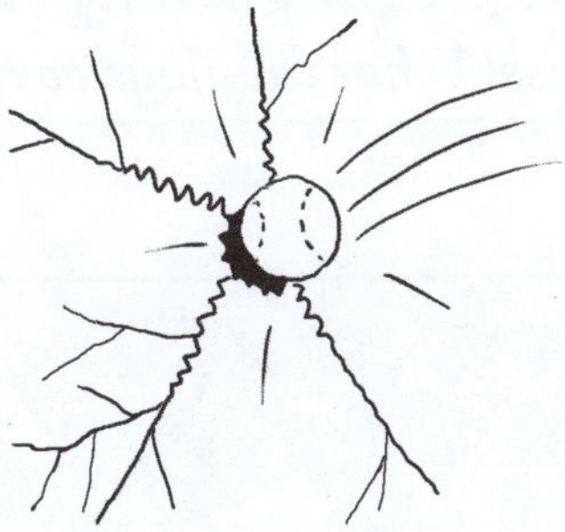

____

____

3 Draw a picture to match these exclamations.

Wow! Just what I wanted!	Everybody stand back!

Sentences - Exclamations

Many sentences express sudden surprise, joy, anger or danger. They are called exclamations. They are marked by an exclamation mark, for example: Stop! Help!
I don't believe it!
What! Late again! Get out!

1 Complete each sentence with a full stop or an exclamation mark. Justify your reasons.

a What? You left your bag on the bus

b I went shopping for a new pair of denim jeans

c What a beautiful day it is

d Dad's going to take us for a drive in his new car

e Let's go roller skating on Saturday afternoon

f What a wonderful beach

Exclamation marks also follow words and phrases expressing strong emotion, for example: *Ouch! Oops! Man overboard! My goodness! What fabulous earrings!*

2 Write an exclamatory sentence for each picture.

3 Illustrate these exclamations.

That's so funny!

Stand back!

WORK SHEET 48

Sentences in Dialogue

Sentences can record the speech of one person to another. This is called dialogue, for example:

"I went to Srinagar last week," said Maya.

"Was it cold there?" asked Karan.

Speech is written in **present, past** or **future** tense.

Speech marks are placed around the spoken words.

1 Highlight the spoken words in this dialogue.

"Dad's taking us to Goa by train this holiday," said Pooja excitedly. "Where are you going, Rahul?"

"We're going to stay in a resort, just south of Mumbai," Rahul replied. "We'll be right beside the beach."

"That sounds like fun too," said Pooja. "We should get some great photos."

"Yeah, Mum has just bought a digital camera and she wants to try it out,"
said Rahul. Then he smiled, "She's not very good with techno things, though."

**2 Write the spoken words given below in the empty boxes.
Go back and put speech marks around the spoken words.**

a ______________________ begged Kavita.

b ______________________ cried Baby Bear.

c ______________________ the waiter said politely.

d ______________________ the captain warned his team.

e ______________________ I said, wiping my hands on my apron.

Who didn't do their homework?	Let me show you the menu
Please come to the movies with me	Who has been sleeping in my bed?
We'll need to score an early goal	Just stir in the flour slowly

WORK SHEET 49

Sentences in Dialogue

Spoken words are separated from unspoken words by a comma, question mark or exclamation mark. For example: "Let's take the dog for a walk," said Tom. "Where do you want to go?" asked Jimmy.

1 Punctuate these questions and answers.

Highlight the spoken words.

Put speech marks around the spoken words.

Separate the spoken words from the unspoken words.

a What game do you want to play asked Jasjeev

Why don't we have a game of marbles answered Karan

b Mayank called out has anyone seen my football

No Mayank shouted everyone all together

c Where is the nearest shop asked the man from Africa

It's not far said Jack do you want me to take you

2 Now write a question and answer of your own.

____

____

3 Punctuate this dialogue. (Reminder: NEW speaker has a NEW line.)

How was your first day back at school Aunty Shiela asked

It was great said Sara my teacher's name is Ms Mohan and

I'm sitting beside my best friend

What was the best thing you did today Aunty Shiela asked

Sara said the teacher took photos of all the children she

told us we would be writing a little bit about ourselves

to go in a class book

That sounds interesting said Aunty Shiela

Punctuation

Capital letters are used for:	
• the first word in a sentence.	*Come to the circus with me.*
• proper names.	*Cinderella danced with Prince Charming.*
• the first spoken word in dialogue.	*He said, "Let's play cricket."*
• to emphasise important words.	*You did WHAT?*
Full stops end statements and commands.	*That is a fine straw hat.* *Put it on, please.*
Question marks end questions.	*How long will you be away?*
Exclamation marks end exclamations.	*What! Late again!*
Commas are used:	
• to separate words in a list.	*I like apples, pears, plums and grapes.*
• to separate a beginning phrase.	*Later that day, we went for a swim.*
• to separate a beginning clause.	*When I broke my leg, I used crutches.*
• to separate an embedded phrase.	*Jyoti, waving her umbrella,* *hurried away.*
• to separate an embedded clause.	*My dog, which is old now,* *still does tricks.*
• to separate spoken and unspoken words.	*"A dingo is a wild dog," said Bittoo.*
Speech marks are used around spoken words.	*"Dinner is on the table," called Bani.* *"Thank you," Jyoti replied.* ***Remember: NEW speaker NEW line.***
Apostrophes are used:	
• with nouns to show possession.	*Karan's toys; dog's collar;* *teachers' staffroom*
• to contract pronouns and helping verbs.	*I've packed lunch. You're invited.* *It's fun.*
• to contract helping verbs and negatives.	*He can't swim. I couldn't sing.* *Don't shout.*

Punctuation

Punctuation establishes the sense of a sentence. It helps us understand where to pause and indicates where to stop.

1 Punctuate the following dialogue.

What do you know about bert hinkler the teacher asked
I think he flew solo from England to Australia replied sara
Yes indeed the teacher nodded do you know when that was
It was in 1928 and it took him sixteen days said jeff confidently
The teacher nodded did you know he died while attempting a second flight

____
____
____
____
____
____
____

2 Insert a comma in the correct place.

Are you going home Monali?
b Dad can you give me a sweet?
c Make a note for me please.
d The man in the khaki dress is Babulal the policeman.
e Yes I saw Neha in the market.
f Please bring apples oranges and some flowers from the market.

3 Punctuate the following passage.

After fighting many wars Alexander was on his way home when suddenly he caught fever He was surrounded by anxious doctors ministers and commanders of his army turning to them he said is there anyone who can give me a few healthy days I will give him half my kingdom in exchange before I die I want to meet my mother

Idioms

An idiom is a form of expression that has a meaning not deducible from those of the individual words in the expression.

What does the picture show you?

It shows you apples in the eyes. But this is not what the idiom 'apple of one's eye' means. It means something deeper. When we say 'apple of one's eye' it means 'a favoured person'.

1 Given below are a few common idioms. Use any two to make sentences.

a bad egg—a worthless person

to keep the ball rolling—to keep things going

to receive with open arms—to welcome cordially

to build castles in the air—to day dream

to take up arms—to go to war

____

____

____

____

2 Choose the correct idiom to fill in the blanks.

a School would be a ____________________ without tests and homework.

apple of one's eye

bed of roses

a bad egg

b Exhausted from my long hike through the park, I decided to __________.

hit the hay

take up arms

bed of roses

Idioms

Some common idioms are—cough up, wet blanket, spill the beans, make ends meet, smell a rat **and** out of the woods.

1 Given below are some common idioms. Choose their correct meanings from the list on the right.

be par for the course	find compromises
give the game away	make people feel relaxed with each other
give and take	do something in a way that will give good results
have it in for	choose what you want
know inside out	be determined to hurt or criticise
break the ice	spoil a secret surprise or joke
take your pick	know everything about a subject
behind closed doors	be condescending
be in two minds	an exclamation of admiration
hats off to	be undecided
full of holes	spontaneously
off the cuff	awkward in handling things
talk down to	privately or secretly
all thumbs	including many flaws

Phrases

A phrase is a group of words without a subject. A phrase becomes a sentence when we add a verb or subject to it.

A phrase is a group of words without a verb or subject, often beginning with a preposition.
A phrase is different from a sentence. It does not begin with a capital letter, has no punctuation and no verb.
For example: in the garden, up the chimney, at home, by your watch
A phrase become a sentence when we add a verb to it.

1 Match the following to make complete sentences.

a	I use a pencil	to drink water.
b	I need a bed	to tie the papers.
c	She uses a glass	to cut with.
d	They want sheets	in the day.
e	We use a knife	with our parents.
f	He needs a string	to write with.
g	We go out	of paper.
h	Owls sleep	to sleep on.

2 Complete the following sentences using meaningful phrases.
The first one is done for you.

a Little Jack Horner <u>sat in a corner</u>.

b The shopkeeper is placing ______________________.

c __________________ bounced on the bed.

d What is the time ____________________?

e We buy stamps ________________.

f Birds begin to sing ____________.

Prefixes and Suffixes

A prefix is a word part added to the beginning of a word. Some words can have several different prefixes, forming new words with very different meanings. Suffixes are word endings that change the grammar of the word.

Suffixes **–er**, **-or**, **-ist** form nouns.
For example: dance-dancer; sail-sailor; violin-violinist
Suffixes **–ion** and **–ance** also form nouns.
For example: revise-revision; attend-attendance
Suffixes **–en**, **-ate** and **–ify** indicate verbs.
For example: identity-identify; tough-toughen
Some of the common suffixes are **–ress**, **-ness**, **-er**, **-es**, **-ed**, **-ly**, **-est**
For example: act-actress, heavy–heaviness, widow-widower, hero-heroes, show-showed, wise-wisely

1 Add suffixes and rewrite the following words.

reach	____________	fast	____________
bright	____________	box	____________
long	____________	farther	____________
finish	____________	soon	____________
gradual	____________	mix	____________

2 Fill in the blanks using the suffixes **–able** or **-ible**.

a Madan promised to take kavita to a fashion____________ restaurant.

b Rahul is an elig ____________ bachelor.

c I wish my teachers were more flex ____________.

d It is good to have a depend ____________ friend.

e Daddy found a suit ____________ match for my sister.

f Is this dress comfort ____________?

g I saw a movie about an invis ____________ man.

Prefixes

A prefix is a word part added to the beginning of a word. Some words can have several different prefixes, forming new words with very different meanings.
For example: discover, recover, uncover; downplay, replay, display.

1 Highlight the correct word in brackets.

a The explorer (uncovered, discovered) a swift-flowing river.

b The newspaper keeps everybody (deformed, informed).

c A (triangle, rectangle) has four sides.

d The concert was (underway, subway) by 7:30.

e The block of wood was soon (converted, diverted) into a work of art.

f After repairs, the electrician (disconnected, reconnected) the power supply.

2 Before and after.
Select a word from the boxes below and write it in each sentence.

a The stockman will get together his cattle this [ ].

b I usually buy [ ] meat.

c Dinosaurs are [ ] creatures.

d Did the weather report [ ] a thunderstorm?

e The earthquake was followed by many [ ].

f We bought Uncle Kapoor a bottle of [ ] for his birthday.

prehistoric	aftershave	preposition	aftershocks
prepacked	afterthought	afternoon	predict

Composition Paragraph

A paragraph is a group of sentences written around a central theme.

A paragraph consists of a number of sentences revolving around one idea.
For example: if we want to write a paragraph on an apple, we need to describe it—its colour, shape, size.
A number of paragraphs makes up a composition.
For example: if we were to write a composition on an apple, the first paragraph would be the introduction (what is an apple), the following paragraph would describe the apple, the third paragraph would tell us where apples are grown, in which season. In the final paragraph or the conclusion we could write why we need to eat apples and what are its benefits for health.

1 Write a paragraph on one of the following:
My House
My Friend

____

____

____

____

____

____

____

____

____

____

____

Composition

My Birthday Party

1 Write a composition on My Birthday Party. You can use the following clues.

Paragraph I: Introduction, when do you plan to celebrate the party?
Paragraph 2: Planning for the party, making a list of invitees, decorations, who will help you, what dress will you wear?
Paragraph 3: Who all came, cutting the cake (its shape and flavour), presents you received
Paragraph 4: Opening your presents and thanking your parents.

Composition Letter Writing

Letters are used for formal and informal communication.

Letters are a good way of keeping in touch with people. At one time they were the main means of communication. Now we have telephone, the Internet and fast travel. Letters are still an important means to communicate.

Learn how to write a letter.

Keep the following in mind while writing a letter:

- Your address at the top right-hand side.
- Date below your address.
- Name of the person you are writing the letter to.
- Address of the person on the envelope.
- If it is an informal letter, write your name at the bottom right-hand side.
- If you are writing to a friend, you address by writing Dear _______
- If you are writing to an elder, you write Dear mummy/uncle, or whatever the relationship may be.
- Start writing a letter away from the margin and in paragraph form.

For example:

Dear Maria,

I was happy to receive your letter.

- You can end the letter in many ways, depending on who you are writing to.
  For example: Your loving niece, yours lovingly/affectionately.

1 Write a letter on any one of the following:

- To your friend telling him/her how you celebrated your birthday.
- To your uncle thanking him for the good time you had with him during the holidays.

WORK SHEET 59

Composition

Letter Writing

1 Draw an envelope, write the name and address. Do not forget to write the pin code of the city and draw a stamp.

Composition
Diary Writing

Diary entries are a recap of the day's events.
A diary is generally written in first person.

What does a diary do? It helps you to keep your memories alive. It is like a friend with whom you can share all your feelings—happy or sad.

While writing a diary remember to:

- Write the date.
- Write in brief all that happened during the day — at home, in school and anywhere else that you may have gone.
- Language should be simple and informal.
- You may begin by writing the date or you may address the diary as a friend.

Sample

Date: 15 Dec 2008

Dear Diary,

What a memorable day it has been for me today! It was our sports day and I came first in the Lemon Race. Imagine the lemon did not fall from the spoon even once.

Happy but nervous when my name was called out as the prizewinner, I went up the stage to receive my certificate and medal from the chief guest, the Governor of Delhi.

My parents took leave from office. They must have felt so proud of me just as I am of myself!

1 Write a diary entry on any of the following:

The day the results were declared

My first day of summer holidays

The day my pet arrived

____

____

____

____

____

____

____

____

WORK SHEET 61

Composition
Poster Writing

A clear and concise poster, meant for the right audience, is important to convey the message of the poster.

A poster is a large printed picture or notice used for decoration or advertisement.

For example:

SPEED THRILLS BUT KILLS

Remember the following when making a poster.

- It should be brief.
- The message should be clear.
- The colours used should be bright and eye-catching.

1 Make a poster to depict any two of the following:

Clean teeth

Goa as a beautiful tourist spot

Launching a new product

Composition Story Writing

A story is based on a real or an imaginary event. A story usually has a beginning, a middle and an end.

Reading stories is fun. Writing stories can be fun too.
While writing a story:

- Jot down the points or thoughts, organize them after writing an outline.
- Understand what the story is about—decide the characters.
- Write as you would write a composition—with an introduction, main body and an end or conclusion.
- Make the story interesting by having real-life characters doing exciting and fascinating things.
- Generally stories are written in past tense.
- Give a suitable title to the story.

Example
Outline
Moby – dog – lucky charm – bumped into Toby – both apologised – paint fell – Moby shows Toby lucky charm – breaks – taking off – Toby takes for repair – Moby – supermarket – cancel order – buys raffle ticket – wins hamper – also gets prizes for 100th customer of the day – salesperson asks reason for coming to market – cancel order

Lucky Charm

One day Moby was feeling lucky because he was wearing an amulet around his neck.
He bumped into Toby who was carrying a box of paint. The paint fell and spill all over the floor. Both apologized to each other.

"Don't worry, Toby, I'd be surprised if you found a single spot of paint on my body," said Toby.

"How can you be so sure?" asked Toby.

"That's because I am wearing a lucky charm," replied Moby. "Only good luck can come to me."

"Show it to me please," pleaded Toby.

While taking off the charm, it broke. Toby felt guilty that it was because of him that the charm broke. He took it from Moby and offered to get it repaired.

Composition
Story Writing

Moby went to the market. He bought a raffle ticket. It was his lucky prize-winning number, 13.

He was awarded a hamper of groceries. His name was called out and he received several gifts, such as an oven and a toaster, for being the hundredth customer of the day.

The owner of the supermarket asked him what he had come to buy. Moby replied, "I came here to cancel my order for repairing the lucky charm."

Story writing can also be done with the help of pictures. This is known as picture story writing.

1 Write a short story using the following picture clue.

WORK SHEET 63

Composition

Book Review

Do you read books? Have you ever chosen to read a book after reading its review? What is a book review?

A book review tells us what the book is about, why it should be read and the interesting features of the book.

Tips on writing a book review:

- Give the title and the author of the book.
- Write an interesting introduction that makes the reader want to read on.
- Give a short outline about the plot (what happens) of the book.
- Write about your favourite part using adjectives.
- Write an exciting ending without telling the reader the end of the book!

Sample book review

The book I read: *Alice in Wonderland* by Lewis Carroll

This book tells about the many exciting adventures of Alice in an extraordinary place called Wonderland. In Wonderland, anything can happen—animals talk, a deck of cards comes to life. Alice meets a big, white talking rabbit and follows him down and down into the magical Wonderland. This book was first published in 1865 and has since then been an all-time favourite. Read the book to find out about the other odd things in store for Alice in Wonderland.

I would give it a gold star.

Composition

Book Review

1 **Try writing a book review using the following format.**

Book title:
Author:
The character you liked the best:
What went wrong:
How the problem was solved:
The funniest part:
The saddest part:
The sort of reader who would like this book:
I would give it a gold/silver/bronze medal:

Revision 3

1 Fill in the blanks with suitable prepositions.

a I met my friends ______ the railway station.

b I decided not ______ move from the platform.

c He had no time for the people _____ the valley.

d She lived _______ her aunt.

e ______ she left, the boys had a party.

f She peeped ______ the shed.

g My aunty sat ______ her.

h Which country are you _______?

i Mr Gupta prefers tea _______ coffee.

j When do you leave _______ Cochin?

k Gita is married ______ a very handsome man.

2 Join the following sentences using appropriate conjunctions.

a The bucket was heavy. He could not lift it.

____

b Two rag pickers passed that way. They were looking for junk that they could sell.

____

c She ran fast. She wanted to catch the bus.

____

d Shanti rang the bell. Mini opened it.

____

3 Read the following sentences and underline the subject part in green and the predicate part in red. Circle the subject, object and verb in green, red and blue, respectively.

a Who says we cannot do this?

b Grandfather climbed up the stairs.

c The old man was upset at her remarks.

d The tsunami took away our village.

e Can you hear the lions roaring?

f Granny cannot hear soft sounds.

Revision 3

4 Change the following into positive sentences.

a Akbar did not go to the forest.

____

b Do not go forward.

____

c We have decided not to go to the party.

____

d She did not know anyone.

____

5 Identify the types of sentences.

a She has come from Mumbai. ______________

b Who dropped you to school? ______________

c Gouri said she looked proud. ______________

d That sure is fun! ______________

e Are you frightened or anxious? ______________

f Kindly allow me to go out. ______________

g My mother has got a new job. ______________

h Please come over to my house this afternoon. ______________

i Hello! I am fine! ______________

j They are getting ready for a party. ______________

6 Punctuate the following.

dear ms chopra,

my latest work Cinderella received a lot of attention with my help she married prince Longfellow and moved into essel castle

Revision 3

7 Choose the correct word to fill in the blanks.

a The anxious father (paced paste) the floor.

b Ointment will help to (heel heal) the wound.

c She was a (guessed guest) at the wedding.

d They all (new knew) the answer to the first question.

e If you (break brake) the vase, you must buy me another one.

f We (eight ate) hot, chocolate muffins.

g The (see sea)side resort was beautifully designed.

8 Add a suffix or a prefix.

a Stop_____

b _____secure

c Full_____

d Beautiful_____

e _____happy

f Strong_____

9 Make ten words from the word BEAUTIFUL.

_____________ _____________ _____________

_____________ _____________ _____________

_____________ _____________ _____________

10 Write a diary entry on a rainy Sunday.

11 Write a paragraph on "The day I broke the flower vase".

WORD BANKS Prefixes

change word meaning

a- *on, in, into, to*	ab- *off, away, from*	ad- *direction, addition*	after- *afterwards*	ante- *before in space/time*
aboard	abduct	adjacent	afterburner	antebellum
about	abhor	adjourn	afterimage	antecedent
adrift	abnormal	adjudicate	afterlife	antechamber
afoot	abort	adjust	aftermath	antedated
alight	absent	admire	afternoon	antelope
along	absolute	admit	aftershave	antemeridian
aloud	absolve	advance	aftershock	antemundane
among	absorb	advantage	aftertaste	antenatal
anew	abstain	adversity	afterthought	anterior
away	abstract	advocate	afterwards	anteroom

anti- *before in space/time*	arch- *first, chief*	auto- *self*	bene- *well*	bi- *two*
antibiotic	arch fiend	autobiography	benediction	bicentenary
anticlimax	arch rival	autocrat	benedictory	bicycle
anticlockwise	arch villain	autocue	benefaction	biennial
antidote	archangel	autograph	benefactor	bifocal
antifreeze	archbishop	autoharp	benefice	bilingual
antigovernment	archdeacon	automatic	beneficial	binoculars
antioxidant	archduchess	automaton	beneficiary	biped
antiperspirant	archduke	automobile	benefit	biplane
antisocial	archenemy	autopilot	benevolence	bipolar
antivenene	archetype	autosuggestion	benevolent	bisect

circum- *round*	co- *association/action*	com- *with, jointly*	con- *with, jointly, in combination*	contra- *opposite/opposing*
circumference	coagulate	combination	concentrate	contraband
circumfluent	coaxial	combine	condition	contrabass
circumlocutory	co-dependence	combustion	confide	contraception
circumnavigate	coerce	commence	congenial	contraceptive
circumscribe	coexist	commute	congratulate	contradict
circumspect	cohabit	complacent	connect	contralto
circumstance	cohesive	complain	consent	contravene
circumstantial	coincidence	complete	consider	
circumstantiate	cooperate	compose	converge	
circumvent	coordinate	compute	convince	

WORD BANKS Prefixes
change word meaning

counter- *contrary to*	**de-** *separation, negation, reversal*	**di-** *through, between, across, by*	**dis-** *away, apart, reversing effect*	**down-** *downwards*
counteract	debrief	digest	disagree	downfall
counterattack	decay	digress	disappear	downgrade
counterbalance	decide	dilate	disband	downhearted
counterintelligence	decompose	dilute	discard	downhill
countermand	deduct	dimension	discourage	downpipe
counteroffensive	delay	direct	discover	downpour
counterpart	depend	divergent	dislocate	downstairs
countersign	destroy	divert	disobey	downstream
countersink	determine	divest	displace	downtown
counterweight	develop	divulge	dissolve	downtrodden

dys- *difficulty, poor condition*	**e-** *variant of ex-*	**en-** *in, into*	**epi-** *near, to, against, above, after, in addition to*	**eu-** *good, well*
dyscalculia	elaborate	enable	epicentre	eucalypt
dysentery	electric	enchant	epicure	Eucharist
dysfunctional	emerge	encircle	epidemic	euchre
dysgenic	enormous	encourage	epidermis	eulogy
dyslexia	eradicate	encroach	epigram	eunuch
dyspepsia	erase	enforce	epilogue	euphonium
dysphasia	erect	engulf	episode	eureka
dysphonic	evacuate	enlighten	epitaph	eurhythmic
dysphoria	evaluate	enliven	epithet	Europe
dysplasia	evolve	entreat	epitome	euthanasia

ex- *from, out of, utterly, thoroughly*	**extra-** *beyond, outside, besides*	**fore-** *front, ahead of time*	**hyper-** *over, excess, exaggeration*	**hypo-** *under, less, less than*
excavate	extradite	foreboding	hype	hypoactivity
exclaim	extragalactic	forecast	hyperactive	hypochondriac
exhale	extrajudicial	forefront	hyperbole	hypocrite
explain	extraneous	forego	hypermarket	hypocritical
explore	extraordinary	foreground	hyperphysical	hypodermic
export	extrapolate	forehead	hypersensitive	hypoglycaemia
ex-president	extrasensory	foreshadow	hypersonic	hypotenuse
exterminate	extraterrestrial	foretaste	hyperspace	hypothermia
extreme	extraterritorial	foretell	hypertension	hypothesis
ex-wife	extravagant	forewarn	hyperventilate	hypothetical

WORD BANKS Prefixes

change word meaning

il- *variant of in-*	im- *variant of in-*	in- *not*	inter- *between*	mis- *mistaken, wrong, negation*
illegal illegible illegitimate illicit illiterate illogical ill-timed ill-treat illuminate illustrious	imbalance immature immeasurable immortal immovable impassable impatient impersonal impossible improbable	inaccurate inanimate inappropriate inarticulate incredible inexcusable inexplicable informal invincible invisible	interact interfere interject intermingle international internet interrupt interschool intersect interstate	misbehave miscalculate misfortune mishap misjudge misplace mispronounce misrepresent mistrust misuse
over- *above, beyond*	**para-** *beyond, near, beside, amiss*	**peri-** *around, about, beyond*	**post-** *behind, after*	**pre-** *before, prior to*
overall overbearing overboard overdose overdue overhead overjoyed overlook overrate overtake	parachute paradox paragon paragraph parallel paramedic paramount paranormal paraphernalia paraphrase	perilous perimeter periodic peripatetic peripheral periphery periphrastic periscope peristyle periwinkle	postdate posterity postgraduate posthumous postmeridian pm post-mortem postnatal postpone postposition postscript	precaution precede precooked predict prefix prehistoric prejudge prelude premonition presuppose
pro- *for, before, in favour of*	**re-** *back, again, reversal*	**retro-** *backwards in space and time*	**se-** *setting apart, taking away*	**semi-** *half*
probation proceed profound prognosis program progress prohibit prologue promote pronounce	refer regain relate relight remake remit replay restore resume return	retroactive retrocede retroflex retrograde retrogressive retro-rocket retrorse retrospect retrospective retroversion	secede secluded secrete secure security seduce select semester sequence serene	semicircle semicolon semiconscious semidesert semidetached semifinal semiprecious semiquaver semiskilled semitone

WORD BANKS Prefixes
change word meaning

sub- *under, not quite*	**super-** *above, superior*	**sym-** *variant of syn-*	**syn-** *association (like co-)*	**trans-** *across, beyond*
subcontract subheading submerge subsonic substandard substitute subterranean subtitle subtropical subway	supercharged superimpose superintendent supermarket supernatural supersede superstar superstructure super-tanker supervise	symbol symbolic symmetrical symmetry sympathise sympathy symphony symphysis symposium symptom	synagogue synapsis synchronise synchronous syndicate syndrome synergy syntax synthesis synthesise	transcontinental transfer transform translate translucent transmit transparent transport transpose transverse
tri- *three*	**ultra-** *beyond in space and time*	**un-** *not, opposite to, reversal of state*	**under-** *below – place or situation*	**up-** *upwards*
triangle triceps tricolour tricycle triennial trihedron trilogy trimaran triplets tripod	ultra sensitive ultraconservative ultracritical ultrafilter ultraloyal ultramarine ultraradical ultrasonic ultrasound ultraviolet	unarmed unbeatable unbend unclean undesirable unfold untimely untraceable untruth unusual	underclothes underdog underestimate undergrowth underline undermine underneath undernourished undervalue underweight	update upgrade upheaval uphill uplifted up-market upright upstage upstart upstream

Adjective-forming suffixes

-al	-ive	-ish	-ic	-ent
casual	active	babyish	bombastic	deficient
coastal	attentive	brownish	comic	dependent
lethal	attractive	devilish	domestic	despondent
local	compulsive	foolish	dramatic	efficient
minimal	effective	impish	idiotic	eloquent
occasional	festive	oldish	optimistic	insolent
personal	impulsive	peckish	pessimistic	proficient
regional	negative	Spanish	rustic	prominent
thermal	positive	stylish	static	reverent
usual	sensitive	sweetish	toxic	transient

-ful	-less	-some	-able	-ible
careful	breathless	awesome	agreeable	admissible
cheerful	defenceless	bothersome	changeable	divisible
colourful	fearless	cumbersome	comfortable	edible
doubtful	leaderless	flavoursome	desirable	horrible
fanciful	merciless	gruesome	fashionable	in/visible
helpful	motherless	handsome	miserable	incredible
peaceful	numberless	loathsome	reasonable	possible
powerful	relentless	meddlesome	reliable	responsible
thoughtful	sleepless	tiresome	untraceable	sensible
truthful	timeless	wearisome	workable	terrible

-er -est *comparative/superlative*	-ial	-ous	-ious	y-
calmer calmest	beneficial	adventurous	delicious	fizzy
faster fastest	commercial	continuous	devious	funny
happier happiest	differential	famous	fallacious	greasy
higher highest	influential	generous	gracious	greedy
hotter hottest	official	jealous	illustrious	hungry
longer longest	partial	mountainous	impervious	risky
older oldest	preferential	nervous	malicious	speedy
slower slowest	sequential	perilous	officious	sunny
thicker thickest	superficial	pompous	precious	tasty
thinner thinnest	territorial	venomous	spacious	tricky

WORD BANKS Suffixes
change word grammar

Noun-forming suffixes

-acy	-ant	-ary -ory -ery	-ance	-ence
accuracy	assistant	cemetery	abundance	competence
bureaucracy	attendant	diary	accordance	conference
conspiracy	combatant	dispensary	circumstance	correspondence
democracy	commandant	documentary	distance	dependence
fallacy	confidant	eatery	disturbance	eloquence
intimacy	consonant	factory	elegance	experience
legacy	dependant	infirmary	entrance	inference
lunacy	pedant	mortuary	nuisance	innocence
piracy	pendant	refectory	performance	persistence
privacy	servant	seminary	reluctance	pretence

-ium	-er	-ism	-ist	-ice
aquarium	announcer	communism	dentist	apprentice
auditorium	baker	escapism	egotist	armistice
conservatorium	builder	fanaticism	exhibitionist	cornice
millennium	buyer	fatalism	extremist	in/justice
planetarium	cricketer	favouritism	guitarist	novice
podium	dancer	idealism	opportunist	police
premium	driver	impressionism	racist	practice
solarium	photographer	racism	sadist	prejudice
stadium	teacher	rheumatism	soloist	service
terrarium	trader	unionism	violinistaccomplice	

-cle	-hood	-itis	-ion	-tion
debacle	adulthood	appendicitis	apprehension	collection
icicle	babyhood	arthritis	conclusion	competition
manacle	brotherhood	bronchitis	decision	destination
monocle	childhood	dermatitis	derision	education
oracle	falsehood	fibrositis	illusion	pollution
particle	fatherhood	laryngitis	impression	explanation
pinnacle	motherhood	meningitis	occasion	illustration
receptacle	parenthood	peritonitis	opinion	instruction
spectacle	priesthood	sinusitis	pension	invitation
tentacle	sainthood	tonsillitis	question	recreation